**Matias pau~~~~
contract wi~~ ~~~ ~~~~ ends next week.**"

"Exactly. And if I leave you in the rubble that is going to be...smoldering when all of this comes out, it's going to reflect badly on me. On my company." And she was not a billionaire with generational wealth. She was worried about herself.

"And for a second I thought you cared."

"We have to fix this. We have to... We need a bigger boat."

"I don't know what that means."

"If you have a big shark, you need a bigger boat. That's...that's what I know. This is going to hit the headlines, and it is going to create a sensation. You have to make a bigger sensation."

"I'm listening," he said.

"What would be the biggest thing? The biggest thing..." She turned to him suddenly. "You have to get married."

He stared at her for a moment, long and hard. "You're right, Augusta. I have to get married. And I think I should marry you."

BILLIONAIRE'S BRIDE BARGAIN

MILLIE ADAMS

Harlequin

PRESENTS

**H Harlequin®
PRESENTS™**

ISBN-13: 978-1-335-63151-0

Billionaire's Bride Bargain

Harlequin Enterprises ULC
22 Adelaide St. West, 41st Floor
Toronto, Ontario M5H 4E3, Canada
www.Harlequin.com

Printed in U.S.A.

Recycling programs
for this product may
not exist in your area.

Millie Adams is the very dramatic pseudonym of *New York Times* bestselling author Maisey Yates. Happiest surrounded by yarn, her family and the small woodland creatures she calls pets, she lives in a small house on the edge of the woods, which allows her to escape in the way she loves best—in the pages of a book. She loves intense alpha heroes and the women who dare to go toe-to-toe with them.

Books by Millie Adams

Harlequin Presents

The Billionaire's Baby Negotiation
A Vow to Set the Virgin Free
The Forbidden Bride He Stole
Her Impossible Boss's Baby
Italian's Christmas Acquisition

From Destitute to Diamonds

The Billionaire's Accidental Legacy
The Christmas the Greek Claimed Her

The Diamond Club

Greek's Forbidden Temptation

Visit the Author Profile page
at Harlequin.com for more titles.

To Jackie, Lorraine and Caitlin—long may you roar.

CHAPTER ONE

The Pitbull is on board.

SHE SENT THE text off quickly.

Woof.

That was the response from Irinka, which was *liked* by the rest of the chat.

Auggie, short for Augusta, looked down at her phone and allowed her lips to twitch, just slightly. Then she looked up at her boss and his current companion of choice.

Auggie didn't judge women for associating with Matias.

A light shone upon him.

He was the single most beautiful man Auggie had ever seen. Tall and broad shouldered, with hair black as a raven's wing, and eyes like the night sky. They were different sorts of black, she had always thought.

The raven's wing spoke to the glossy, sleek nature of his hair.

The night sky spoke to the perils of space and the inevitable destruction a woman might face if she were to be pulled into his orbit.

Still, though, she couldn't blame the woman.

Matias was responsible for his own appalling behavior.

Though the media enabled him, in her humble opinion.

Glorious Golden Retriever Matias Balcazar Seen Out and About With New Woman!

Golden retriever, her well-rounded behind.

The man was a pitbull.

He would eat your children.

It was how he'd gotten his nickname in the group text, which was appropriately named Work Wives.

Because Irinka, Lynna and Maude were her work wives. And best friends. They'd started Your Girl Friday five years earlier with nothing but a dream, fantastic organizational skills and determination, and it was thriving now.

They were freelance assistants who operated with the utmost discretion. They assisted the richest of the rich with their lives, from managing their personal affairs—Irinka's specialty—to providing culinary brilliance—Lynna—to the rehabilitation and management of the elaborate grounds of ancient estates—Maude.

Auggie was not as specialized as her friends. She was a wrangler, of sorts. An assistant of all kinds. Currently, for Matias, she was his air stewardess. But he spent all his time jet setting around the world in a private plane, and that meant she functioned as a traveling secretary too.

And whether he knew it or not, she did her best to keep his secrets.

She was—happily—coming to the end of her contract with him. Your Girl Friday wasn't designed to ensnare them into full-time employment for one person. So when a job was all-encompassing it had a hard limit. Six months. But her contract with Matias was only for three.

Praise be.

She could tell the exact moment he perceived her. One of her greatest assets was her ability to function as wallpaper in whichever surroundings she currently occupied.

She was a chameleon.

One who had been spotted by the Pitbull.

She ignored the way that it affected her. The way that her stomach went tight when his dark eyes met hers. For heaven's sake, he had a *woman on his arm*. He was her boss—even if for a set period of time. And she... Well, she knew him. She might well be the only person on the planet who did. The image that they painted of him in the media was laughable.

Matias Javier Hernandez Balcazar, beloved by all, was the son of Javier Balcazar, the most ruthless Spanish billionaire in recent times. A man wholly uninterested in ethics, in kindness, in basic human decency. A conquistador of the modern era, and on and on.

There were really only a couple of things a person needed to know about Matias to know him.

The first was that he could not be told. He did whatever he wanted, whenever he wanted, as befitted his position as a billionaire. The second was that he hated his father. And from those two pieces of information flowed the truth.

The media spun a story of his life that just didn't make sense, not when you had met the real Matias.

Somehow, they saw his entry into his own father's industry as him taking what he had learned and building something with it. Not what it actually was. A cold-eyed attempt at taking over his family business and crushing it. She was certain that was what he was up to.

Of course, everyone imagined that he stood to inherit his father's wealth.

Auggie thought that the truth was perhaps slightly more complicated. Though she didn't have all the details, she knew that the truth of the matter was, Matias was anything but what he seemed.

"Augusta," he said, his accent rolling over the syllables of her name in a way that made her want to purr. "Could you get myself and Charmaine a drink?"

"Of course," she said, smiling like the decorative femme bot she was supposed to be and moving to the bar, anticipating exactly what he would have, and what the lady would be having. It was easy enough. She smiled as she poured his whiskey, and then mixed up an overly sweet drink with cherries in it for Charmaine.

Then she melted away into the background again, while standing quite in plain sight.

She picked up her phone again.

If I see another headline about what a glorious himbo this man is I will punch the next starry-eyed reporter I see.

Oh, come on, don't spoil the public's fascination with him.

This came from Lynna.

I won't, because I signed an NDA, as you know. But I'm just saying, I don't think I have ever met anyone whose public persona is as big of a lie as his.

Maude chimed in.

That can't be true. Billionaires are notorious liars. They're also usually okay with being the glorious bastards they are in full view of the public.

Is he awful?

That was Irinka asking.

No. But he's not what he seems.

At that point, Charmaine and Matias abandoned their drinks and disappeared into the bedroom at the back of the private plane. The really fun part was when Auggie had to accompany the women back to whatever city they had come from, if Matias had long-term work in the city they were landing in. That didn't happen every time, often transfer would be arranged in a different way, or the woman would stay over in the city, but never long-term with Matias. It really was an amazing trip. He managed to be a shameless womanizer who was loved by all. Even the women that he had finished with.

Nobody could hate him.

It made Auggie even more suspicious of him, frankly. Because that was some black magic. Different than the black of his hair. Different than his eyes. A kind of sorcery that she couldn't quite access.

That was the problem with him. He was *interesting*.

When she had taken the job with him she had been so certain that he would be dull. He was the world's favorite boyfriend, as Irinka had pointed out. He had a reputation for being polite, a generous employer, a man who gave extravagant tips to anyone who served him. He was quick with a smile.

But that smile never reached his eyes.

She put her headphones in because she didn't need to hear anything happening in the adjacent room. No, she did not.

She managed communications for Matias while they were in the air, and then did some finessing of his schedule. And once the time was appropriate, she put her ear to the bedroom door. And then she opened it slowly. They were both asleep, in bed. She had become very good at simply not looking at the man. Half-dressed, enjoying the aftermath of his liaison. It wasn't her business. He was allowed to conduct himself in whatever way he chose. But she had something she needed to do.

She snagged the woman's phone off of the nightstand and turned it so that it was held up to her face. Then she flinched, swiping up the screen on the unlocked phone, and going to the photos. There were none taken. Thank God. She had deleted pictures of Matias sleeping from multiple women's phones.

There were no photos, but she could see an email banner pop up with some text.

Once you finish with him, I need you to...

And then it cut off.

She sat there and looked at it. And she felt a vague sense of disquiet. Granted, Charmaine could be getting that email about anyone. In any context.

She might not have told anyone she was having a dirty weekend with a hot billionaire.

Auggie hovered her thumb over the email

app. She had lines, and boundaries. She didn't invade people's privacy. She didn't go through texts, she didn't surf through all the photos, the only thing she tried to do—historically—was keep Matias's penis off the internet.

This went outside the boundaries of that.

Whatever it is, it isn't your business.

She let out a breath, and placed the phone back, gingerly. There were no pictures. That was all that mattered. The rest wasn't her problem and couldn't be.

She snuck back out of the room, and not for the first time, gave thanks that she was nearly at the end of all this.

Matias was so much more work than any man she'd ever contracted for. Usually she found her job a delightful challenge. She liked the freshness of having a new client every few months. Typically, what she was doing was giving extra and specialized help while someone increased workload for a new project, or needed help with some image maintenance during a challenging time.

She wasn't PR. But she often worked alongside a PR person to help with the flow of work, so that the subject of her help would look good, efficient, less stressed, etc.

Working with Matias just made her stressed

half the time. And strung out on his beauty, which was a complication she'd never experienced before.

When the plane landed in Barcelona, both Matias and Charmaine tumbled out of the bedroom. Looking disheveled, but lovely, both of them.

She wondered if Matias would ever settle down, or if he was destined to remain unattached. He seemed to exist in the eternal now, but she knew that wasn't true. Because a man didn't accidentally become as successful as he was. Not even if he came from a rich family. Because he had not used his father's money to get where he was.

There was just more to him. It constantly surprised her how the world was willing to take his enigmatic smile as the truth. To assume that he was simplistic, because he was happy to let them believe so. To trip through life as a man winning at the lowest difficulty setting. Which more than one person had said about him, and he seemed completely happy to take that on the chin. He was… Pleased to let people think he was a fool.

And that, to her, was the most suspicious thing of all.

"Charmaine will be staying in Barcelona

for a couple of days, she wishes to see the offices."

"Oh," Auggie said. "So I won't be making a return trip, then."

That hit her strangely, and she knew it was because of the email.

When you're finished with him...

What had the email said? She was so mad she hadn't read it.

"Are you sure she wants to see your offices?" Auggie asked.

"Yes," he said, looking at her like she was a fool.

Charmaine's eyes clashed with Auggie's, and Auggie knew a moment of deep disquiet. She didn't like the look in the other woman's eyes.

Auggie was a girl's girl. Auggie was all about the freedom and power women had to shag Matias to their heart's content without judgment.

Being a girl's girl, though, meant when she didn't trust a woman, there was a reason.

This was nothing more than a gut feeling, but it was a strong one.

"Matias, can I speak to you for a moment?" she asked.

"No," he said smoothly. "Enjoy the city. I shouldn't need you for a couple of days."

She lifted her brows. "Really."

She didn't like this at all.

"Yes. You only worked for me for three months. I find that I can function just as well without you."

"Indeed." She hesitated. "Matias, I wonder if I should just go to the offices with you?"

"No, that won't be necessary."

Maybe he was a dumb, gorgeous idiot.

She swore Charmaine gave her a small smile before they turned away and began to get off the plane and Auggie was stewing.

She didn't know what Charmaine could do being at Matias's offices, but she just felt… she felt *something* about it.

And it had nothing to do with the fact that every day, every week, Matias got more and more attractive to her.

He was like a beautiful object in an art gallery.

Nice for some, but Auggie couldn't afford him. So she would look, but she would never touch.

She packed up her things and watched as Matias got into a waiting limousine with Charmaine. Auggie was ushered into a town car. She was totally happy with that. Happy with the quiet, and the luxury that surrounded her. She was not happy to be told that she wasn't needed, mostly because she didn't believe it.

The Pitbull is disconcerting.

Why is that? Lynna asked.

Because he has brought a woman to the offices, and he said he doesn't need me.

Well, maybe he is a himbo. Only thinking with the Pitbull downstairs. Perhaps he wants to have her on his desk, Irinka said.

He is most assuredly only thinking with his downstairs brain, but he isn't stupid.

She got to the hotel room that had been reserved for her and set up her computer, and all her peripherals. She opened up Matias's schedule, and her calendar. Then she initiated a video call with the work wives.

"I'm in Barcelona."

"You look fantastic," said Irinka, who was always gorgeous in the most immaculate way.

"Glowing," Maude said. Maude, for her part, had mud on her cheek. She was wearing dungarees, and was standing out in a field.

"Irritated," said Lynna, who was standing in a large, commercial looking kitchen.

"I am irritated. Because he has deviated

from the script, and I don't like it. I'm only glad that this is my last outing with him."

"Your next contract is at least for a shorter amount of time," Lynna said. "And with a slightly less infamous man."

"We need more female clients," Auggie said, feeling full of woe.

"I would be happy to have more female clients," Irinka said, "it's only that men see our pictures and want to hire us. Also, women are happy to break up with their partners on their own. Men are the ones who typically need my services."

Irinka was a dark horse. She always had been. She acted publicly as His Girl Friday's secretary, and their avenue for connection to the rich and elite. But in reality she was a breakup artist for hire, and master of disguise. Her services required discretion, and backdoor connections, and she was an expert at both.

Auggie herself wasn't built for subterfuge. She was too honest. Keeping her opinions to herself when her clients were being ridiculous was hard enough—and also why she spent so much time in their group text.

Lynna was the best chef in the world, in Auggie's opinion. To taste her food was to taste magic. Some women could make a man long for them forever after a night. Lynna did it after a meal.

Maude was a fae thing, more at home in nature than in the city. She had once rescued a mouse from the science lab when they were at uni and had brought it to live in their dorms. Even now, her affinity for nature was her specialty.

Auggie, Lynna and Maude had all been friends since university, even though they were all from very different backgrounds.

Irinka was the illegitimate daughter of a duke, and a rumored Russian spy, and Irinka had inherited wealth, connections and a penchant for mystery. Maude had been an odd girl out, by virtue of her otherworldliness, and Auggie had related to her, because even though it was in a different fashion, Auggie felt like she was from a different world.

The American in the group.

Lynna was from Wales, but raised in Greece, with a wealthy family, who had lost everything while poor Lynna was at university. Her father had died during the horrific aftermath, and all the friends had rallied around Lynna to make sure she could still complete her studies. To make sure she could still have her life.

They'd stayed together after university too—starting His Girl Friday. With their powers combined, like they were Voltron, from the old cartoon. Individually, they were great. Together they were a powerful force. They'd overcome their past adversity and they'd turned it into something successful. Amazing.

Though she wasn't feeling all-powerful at the moment.

Worry nagged at the back of her brain.

"What?" Maude asked.

"I'm just… I don't trust this situation. And I am not his PR person, so this isn't my problem." She thought back to the number of times she had deleted pictures of his body off of women's phones. She had always squinted when she hadn't looked at those photos. Careful not to see more than she should. Also careful to make sure that he didn't end up plastered all over newspapers as naked as the day he was born.

So no, she wasn't his PR person, and he wasn't an *idiot*, but he did make questionable decisions where women were concerned.

"You don't have to take care of him," Lynna said. "It isn't your job. You're supposed to *assist* him. This isn't… Caregiving."

She said it kindly, but it lodged itself firmly in Auggie's chest all the same.

"I know that."

"You have that look about you. That paranoid look, that says you're attaching life or death stakes to this situation, and he is not..."

"I know he isn't my mother," she said. "Also, he isn't my problem after this. But you know, if he gets into a serious situation while I'm working for him, it is not going to help our business."

"What do you think is going to happen?" Maude asked.

"I don't know. I have a bad feeling about that woman. I have a bad feeling about this situation." She just did. Even if she couldn't say why. And Augusta Fremont had learned years ago to trust her intuition.

She was in Barcelona. And he wasn't her responsibility, her friends were right. She wasn't his babysitter. So she was going to go out, and she was going to have paella. She was going to let Matias sort out his own issues.

CHAPTER TWO

WHEN HER PHONE rang at five thirty the next morning she knew an instant shot of regret over taking the night off.

"Hello?"

"Is this Augusta Fremont?"

"Yes?" She rubbed her eyes and rolled over in her large, empty bed. If she was like Matias she would have gone out and found herself a bedmate. She would have batted her eyelashes and seduced a gorgeous Spaniard. But she was not, and she was alone. As per always. Her and her cell phone.

"Augusta Fremont of Your Girl Friday?"

"The very one," she said. She did not tell the woman on the other end of the line that everybody called her Auggie. She had hoped, when she was younger, that the nickname Gus might catch on. It was cuter, in her opinion. But no. She was Auggie forever. Now though, when she thought of the nickname, she heard it in her mother's voice, and it softened things inside of her.

"Do you have a comment to make on the news that Matias Balcazar is a fraud?"

"Excuse me?" she asked.

"Yes. Media outlets received reports this morning from an anonymous source alleging that he has engaged in a years-long corporate espionage campaign which has stolen information from his father, Javier Balcazar, and therefore he has built his image on lies."

"It isn't true," she said, sitting up and pushing her brown hair out of her face. "I know that for a fact. Matias is a self-made man whose reputation as such is very important to him. I've spent a great deal of time with him, and I can tell you, he never even mentions his father."

"Well, the evidence that was faxed to us this morning is quite compelling. It doesn't really matter whether you have a comment or not, the story is going to run everywhere."

"Expect a cease-and-desist," she said, hanging up the phone. She was panicking. Not so much because she cared about Matias, but because she was so connected with him.

She scrambled out of bed and put her clothes on. She was his keeper. For better or

for worse. And Your Girl Friday was associated with him. His name was going to be
strongly linked to them no matter what, and
if this…

She was immediately spinning stories in
her mind. Even as she was FaceTiming the
work wives.

Irinka was lying in bed, glaring intently
at the camera. Maude was out on a country
road somewhere, she seemed to be walking
a spaniel, but the camera was jiggling wildly,
so it was hard to say.

Lynna was in a chicken coop. "Fresh eggs,"
she commented, lifting a shoulder.

"Well, here are some not fresh eggs. There's
going to be a major scandal connected to the
Pitbull."

"What, did he get caught with his hand in
the honey jar, so to speak?" Irinka asked, rolling onto her back and bringing the phone with
her. She sat up, revealing that she was wearing extremely luxe-looking pajamas.

"I wish. He got…" She covered her face
with her free hand. "Somebody stole something from his office. It was Charmaine. I'm
convinced. So that is some commitment to
the bit, because she definitely slept with him."

"Auggie," Lynna said. "We've all seen him.

It's not really hugely sacrificial for a woman to sleep with him."

"Like you would know," Auggie said.

If Lynna was put out by that shot about her nonexistent love life, she didn't let it show. Instead, she stroked a chicken's head, and stood, holding the phone up toward her face as she began to walk out of the chicken coop area.

Lynna was professionally unbothered.

"I have to fix this. What am I going to do?"

"You're not his publicist," Irinka pointed out. "She needs to get involved with this."

"But they called me. They called me in the morning, and they asked if I was Augusta Fremont of Your Girl Friday. And I am. We are all Your Girl Friday. If my most prominent client that I have ever had goes down in flames while I'm embedded in his life like this…"

"You need to be embedded in fixing it," Maude said, red-cheeked in the cold English air.

"Right. I do. You're right. I have to fix it. We built this business ourselves. And I can't count on anyone else to do this. Not a publicist, who thinks that the best way to shape his image is to paint him as an idiot. This just makes him look even more stupid."

"He's probably not *stupid*," Maude said thoughtfully. "It's just that he's egotistical. Overconfidence gets beagles into a lot of trouble also."

"He's not a beagle," she said.

"No, I know that," Maude said.

Auggie decided to let that go. "Remember in *Jaws*," Irinka said.

"I don't," Auggie said. "I don't share your affinity for shark movies."

"Well," Irinka said. "In *Jaws*, when they actually see the size of the shark, they realize they need a bigger boat. If you can't have a smaller shark, get a bigger boat."

"I'm not following," Auggie said.

"If there's a big headline, make a bigger one."

"Well, first I need to talk to him, I need to find out what's going on. I need to find out if there's any truth to this. Because we can always squash it with the truth."

Irinka laughed, the sound like a fork on crystal, and sat straight up in bed. "Are you that naïve, Auggie? You can't fix lies with the truth. Because there's a certain point where the truth doesn't matter. That's not what the public wants. They want a narrative. The idea that he might've done something underhanded to gain his success is a fantastic narrative, because you know he has secret haters."

"He doesn't. Everybody loves him. A light shines upon him. He is the most beautiful man in the world."

"He has slept with more women than most men have ever *met*," Irinka persisted. "He's rich, he's gorgeous, and people love to watch a guy like that fall. They really do."

"You think they're going to turn on him."

"I think that's what mobs do," Irinka said.

"Hedgehogs also do that," Maude said.

No one said anything in response.

"Okay," Auggie said. "I'll keep you posted. I have to go to... Wherever he's at."

"Good luck," Lynna said.

"We all need it," Auggie said, hanging up the phone. She took a couple of deep breaths and looked in the mirror. She was not quite as done up as she would like. But there were things she had to do. Very important things.

And then she was off like a hare, making a beeline straight for the residence that he kept in Barcelona. The address was in her files, and she had gotten a car before even finding it.

The whole drive she became more and more agitated. She was supposed to be finished with him soon and this was a logistical nightmare.

She had been nice, and she had been silent, and she had been the wallpaper, and look where it had gotten them both.

He was going to be reamed for this. She wasn't going to handle him gently here. She had tried to warn him when he'd gotten off the plane and he hadn't listened.

When she was dumped summarily out onto the sidewalk, she went to the wrought iron gates that led to a winding driveway, and pressed a button on the intercom. She was fueled by indignation and outrage. "Hello, Augusta Fremont is here to see Mr. Balcazar."

She did not expect Matias himself to respond to the intercom. "Of course you may enter, Augusta."

The gates swung open toward her, and she took two hopping steps backward, and then skittered inside, running up the steeply graded driveway toward the most opulent hacienda she had ever seen in her life. Tucked into the hills, with bright pink flowers spiraling all around, vines growing up a tall wall that encircled the outside of the stucco masterpiece. The red-tiled roof gleamed in the early morning sun, and Auggie had never been so full of

MILLIE ADAMS   31

hate. She leaned against the front door, trying to catch her breath. And then it opened, and she nearly tumbled inside, and right into the solid wall of Matias's body.

She gasped, and lunged backward. "You are in a crisis," she said.

His dark brows lifted, and he looked around. "Am I? I do not see a crisis anywhere in the vicinity."

"Of course you don't. Because it's not printed yet. You took Charmaine to the office, didn't you?"

"She wished to see the headquarters."

"She wished to do some digging. I'm convinced. I saw an email on her phone…"

"You were on her phone?"

"I always check their phones, Matias," she said, not breaking eye contact with him. "For photographs of your penis."

He looked shocked. Not by the word *penis*, she supposed. But by her pushing back against him. She didn't care. She had absolutely nothing to lose in this moment. She pinched the bridge of her nose and continued.

"I got a call from a media outlet this morning claiming that they received evidence that you engaged in corporate espionage."

And that was when the smile melted right off his face. "What?"

"They're claiming that you've been stealing from your father. *Everything*. Leads, information. I don't know what all. I'm not an expert in corporate espionage, I am an expert in... Knowing that this is a very bad thing."

"I have taken nothing from my father," he said, his voice suddenly hard.

"Well, they seem to think that you did. And supposedly there's evidence to that effect."

"Why do you think it was Charmaine?"

"I picked up her phone, and there was an email preview. It said, When you're done with him... I didn't read the rest because that isn't in my scope, but when you said you were taking her to the offices, it got my antennae up. I tried to get you stay back and talk to me, but you didn't."

"No," he said. "I didn't, but you didn't say you were worried she was going to do something nefarious."

"I didn't know what she was going to do, because I didn't know what she might find evidence of at your offices, Matias." That he might be guilty of corporate espionage was a problem, she supposed. It was just that she didn't care. Trying to apply ethics to billionaires was stupid, and in her opinion, based on everything she knew, his father was the worst, so what did it matter if he took some of the old man's trade secrets?

On moral grounds, she couldn't care less if she tried.

But if he was guilty, it was a complication in the practical sense.

He paused for a moment. "Why do you care?"

"What do you mean, *why do I care*?"

"Your contract with me ends next week."

"Exactly. And if I leave you in the rubble that is going to be… Smoldering when all of this comes out, it's going to reflect badly on me. On my company." And she was not a billionaire with generational wealth. She was worried about herself.

"And for a second I thought you cared."

Her phone buzzed and she pulled it out of her pocket.

Did you find the Pitbull?

His eyes glanced downward, and he caught the message on her lock screen. She put it away quickly.

"The Pitbull?" he asked.

"You have a code name, obviously, with my coworkers. Because we have to talk about logistics, but of course we're discreet." She gritted her teeth and did not say: unlike you.

"You call me a pitbull because you find me dangerous?"

Well, to his point, she had a week left on her contract with him. And no reason not to tell him exactly what she felt.

"I call you a pitbull, because pitbulls are *silly*, and *emotional*, and make very abrupt reactionary choices. That is what makes them dangerous, not their aggression. And apparently it's what makes you dangerous too."

"I am not *silly*," he said, the hardness in his eyes that she had never seen before.

"Well, you're going to have to do some work to prove that to me."

"I have nothing to prove to you Augusta. If you find me inconvenient, then leave."

"No. We have to fix this. We have to… We need a bigger boat."

"I don't know what that means."

"If you have a big shark, you need a bigger boat. That's… That's what I know. This is going to hit the headlines, and it is going to create a sensation. You have to make a bigger sensation."

"I'm listening."

"What would be the biggest thing. The biggest thing…"

She turned to him suddenly. "You have to get married."

He stared at her for a moment, long and hard. "You're right, Augusta. I have to get married. And I think I should marry you."

CHAPTER THREE

FOR THE FIRST time Matias realized that he might have taken this too far.

He could have ruined his father in a variety of ways. He had decided to do it with a smile on his face. Because one thing Javier Balcazar had been very clear on when he was in the process of trying to bend his children to his will, was that you had to be ruthless to be successful.

You could not be kind. You could not give love. You could not receive love. You had to show no weakness, no happiness, no zeal for life.

So when Matias had made the decision that he was going to start a business competing with his own father and ultimately, absorb his father's company, he'd made the decision to cultivate a public persona that was opposite to Javier in every way.

To prove he was, and always had been, wrong in every way.

That he was cruel because he liked it, not because he had to be.

That he could have been a good father if he weren't a bad man.

Matias had thought that he was playing a game with his playboy persona. He had been certain of it, in fact. Auggie might call him the Pitbull, but he felt more accurately, biblically, even, he was a wolf in sheep's clothing.

Innocent until proven otherwise.

But he had gotten to the point where he had let his guard down, where he had lost himself so much behind the polished veneer of playboy that he had made the sort of miscalculation that meant he had allowed someone to gain access to information about him, then he had retreated further beyond the veil than he had imagined.

The path was set. He had walked it for so long he didn't have to think about the destination.

Maybe that was the problem. This life, building wealth, acting like nothing mattered, taking a new woman to bed nearly every night, it was its own all-consuming endeavor. He never paused to think, because he never had to. He had, in the beginning. He had decided, after Seraphina's funeral that he would be everything his father had never been. That he would take his father's hallowed name and twist it into something different. That he would style himself as an entirely new man, and that he would exceed his father's success by more money, and more notoriety than the other man could ever fathom. He had never stolen from him. He had never needed to. Whatever Charmaine had found... It wasn't what she thought it was.

But he supposed that didn't matter. Public perception was what mattered.

His legacy was what mattered. Not in the way his father saw it, no, quite the opposite. What he wanted was to prove the old man useless, obsolete. His methods an exercise in pointless cruelty, and if he or anyone else believed that he had achieved his success by stealing from a man he despised he would feel like a victory had been handed to Javier.

He would not allow it.

"Me?"

He looked at Augusta. She had been his assistant, his flight attendant, for the past three months. She had practiced utmost discretion in all things. He practically lived on his jet, and the person who attended him there was the one that he saw most of anyone in his life.

She was beautiful, but in an almost nondescript way. Though, this morning, there was something different about her.

Perhaps it was the high color on her cheeks, the way that she was breathing hard. Perhaps it was that her long brown hair was loose around her shoulders, and wild from her running up the driveway.

Perhaps it was that she had no makeup on. Usually, she had a full face of it, very natural, but very polished.

There was something intimate about seeing her like this. He imagined not many did.

That was unimportant.

Her beauty was secondary to everything else. Though, he did feel that if he was going to show up with a random fiancée, she had to be believably beautiful.

Also, he had spent so much time with her over the last three months, and that was well documented.

There would of course, be women who tried to sell stories of him sleeping with them on the plane. There was nothing he could do about that. He didn't ask women to sign

NDAs. Often, his treatment of them earned him respect even after they parted.

They didn't know him. Of course they didn't. But the performance he put on with them was a pleasant one.

If he could say one thing for the way he chose to live his life it was that he didn't cause harm without intending to.

And he would never hurt the innocent.

The guilty, on the other hand…

"We will have to come up with a convincing story, obviously," he said.

She blinked, her mouth dropping open. "About what exactly?"

"There have been witnesses," he said. "To my being in the same space as you while enjoying the company of another woman."

"Well, and maybe your plan is crazy," she said. "Did you ever stop to think of that?"

"No. Because it must be a woman that I have spent significant time with, and there is no one else."

"Well… Obviously we just got together then," she said. He could see the brightness in her eyes, a frantic thought process turning there. "It can work. So yes, there have been other women, but we were trying to keep things professional."

"Obviously. Because we have a contract."

"It's up next week," she said.

"Too long," he said. "We have to get the news out immediately. We almost have to make it look as if this is a backlash to our announcement. We have no time."

He picked up his phone and texted his PR firm. "There. I told them that they need to see the story that we are engaged. We will supply photographs within the next few hours, but we need the rumors to get out now."

"This is… Well, this is utterly unhinged," she said, flexing her hands like little claws, looking extremely twitchy.

An odd thing, because Auggie had, in his view, always been polished and calm. But she'd shown up here in a rage he'd never seen before, and had not seemed to take a full breath since.

"Very few things matter to me, Augusta. But one is that I extricate myself from my father's legacy, and I will not have a narrative dominating the media that I have stolen my success from him. My father is a horrible man."

"I got the feeling that you didn't like him very much."

Few people spent large amounts of time in

his presence. He was always on the move. But he wasn't shocked that Auggie had picked up on that after being around him so frequently these past months. Even with his most polished veneer on he never said a nice thing about Javier Balcazar.

She'd been present when his father had called on a couple of occasions. His father only ever called to remind Matias of the past. He only ever did it to drip poison into his ear, and he knew in those moments his veneer... slipped.

"An understatement," he said. "I hate my father. I hate him with every fiber of my being. I hope that he dies an old, lonely man. I wish him a long life only so that time can begin to twist everything that he is so proud of. That he might lose control of everything, including his body, so that he can know what it was like to grow up in his shadow. I despise my father," he said, all of the darkness in him rising up to the surface. "And this is the most appalling claim that could've ever been made against me."

"Do you think perhaps it's worth combating the rumors?"

"No," he said, his voice rough. "If we deny them, it cannot be right away. And it must be with the sort of attitude that suggests I find the rumors beneath me. I am living my life."

"They aren't true, though," she said.

"No," he said. "They're not true. I keep information on my father's company, but it isn't to steal from him. It's to keep tabs on him."

"You have stolen information," she said.

"No one will understand why except for me," he said.

"Well, all the world thinks that you're this... Dumb handsome log who sort of charmed his way into success."

"Because it doesn't benefit me to have them think of me otherwise. I like it that my enemies don't see me coming. You know I'm not dumb, Augusta."

"Yes," she said. "I do. Except the whole thing with Charmaine was dumb."

"It was... It was thoughtless. I... I have been playing this part long enough that sometimes I forget."

She shook her head. "I just... The problem is, if we pretend to get engaged, and then eventually we break up, how is that going to reflect on Your Girl Friday."

"We will part as I always do with my exes, Tesoro. Amicably. I remain friends with every woman who has ever graced my bed. I like women. I don't use them out of an abundance of disdain as many do."

"How nice of you," she said.

"Are you mocking me?"

"Yes," she said. "I am. Because you're trying to paint this… This confusing thing that you are, that you're doing, as something that is perfectly normal when it is absolutely not."

"I don't care what normal is," he said. "It has always been about revenge. Always. Do you know what my father wanted from his children? Compliance. He wanted us to be perfect mirrors of him. His daughter had to be angelic and feminine, pure in all ways. And I was to be his right hand. We were not raised with love, affection or care. We were raised under the iron fist of his authority and that does not make for a normal childhood. Therefore, it does not lead to a normal life."

Her eyes darted away from his. "I can understand that."

He very much doubted she could understand it. At least to the degree that she thought. She had no idea what it was like to grow up with a father like his.

Perhaps that wasn't fair. But he did not traffic in fairness.

Also, he trusted her. Even if it made no

sense. But she'd seen him. In more unguarded moments—even if not many—than any other person had in years. She was here. She knew him. She knew this. It had to be her.

"We have to negotiate the terms of this," she said.

"You have already signed an NDA," he said.

"And you will have to sign one as well," she said, her dark eyes boring into his. She was a tiny little thing, but she was determined. He had always seen that quality in her. He had… Liked Auggie from the moment he had met her, though he refused to refer to her by the nickname he had heard the other women at the company call her.

It was a strange name for a small, cute woman. And yet, in some way she exemplified it. But nicknames implied an intimacy that he did not experience with… Anyone.

"If you insist," he said.

"I do. Because if the truth of this came out, then it would be seen as entirely unethical. Already, we are walking a fine line. Because my clients will think that it's possible for me to become sexually involved with them. And…" Her cheeks went scarlet, and when she looked up at him then, he felt an answering tightness in his stomach.

Ridiculous. He'd had sex not twelve hours earlier. With a woman who had betrayed him, no less. Why should he get physically excited by the woman standing in front of him?

Because she interests you. Not the you that you pretend to be. The one that exists underneath.

He ignored that internal voice.

It was true, he was the living embodiment of the duality of man. But he didn't spend a lot of time thinking about that.

It was his ruthlessness that propelled him, it was his charisma that kept him afloat.

There was that very old concept. Being like a duck. Calm on the surface, paddling like hell underneath. He wouldn't compare himself to a duck. Perhaps a shark.

Though the media had chosen to compare him to a golden retriever.

"That's why you call me the Pitbull," he said, suddenly realizing. "Because you know that I'm not what they say."

She rolled her eyes. "Of course I know that. Do you really think you seem like a golden retriever? Like a happy, biddable, people-pleasing family pet?"

"The press seems to think so."

"You're a handsome man. And people love

to apply positive qualities to men, particularly when they're handsome. But I've never thought the description of you seemed at all legitimate. Not even close."

"What is it you see?"

She drew back, just slightly. "I think you're dangerous. I haven't decided quite in what way."

"You think that I might've committed corporate espionage," he said.

"I actually don't. Mostly because you don't seem like a man who is angry that he got caught. I believe you. You're angry because you think stealing from your father is beneath you."

"Yes. But more than that, it defies the very point of… All of this."

"You have to tell me the truth."

"I don't talk about the past."

She sighed heavily, pinching the bridge of her nose. "Let's go into the dining room."

"Why?"

"I need coffee. I got woken up by a reporter demanding to know if I wanted to spill secrets about you. And I ran straight over here to try and fix it. When did Charmaine leave, by the way?"

"She didn't stay the whole night. Women never do."

"Well, undoubtedly not women on your father's payroll."

He growled. "Unconscionable…"

"Why did you let her in?"

"Because I…" He did not like this. Being centered by a tiny little creature. This was how he had lived his life for years. And of course, this was where his father saw weakness. He hadn't believed that it really was a weakness of his. He had thought it was part of the show. And yet, the show and the man had become one and the same. He engaged in the behavior, so what did it matter?—Was it part of a put-on or not? The truth was, he was indiscriminate when it came to taking lovers. His father knew that. And so of course that was the avenue that he took to come at him.

The mistake he had made was that in his disdain he had begun to minimize who his father was. He had shrunk him down to being a cruel man, and because cruelty was something that he despised, he had convinced himself that perhaps the cruelty was stupidity. Of course not. A person could be cruel and yet be horrendously clever. It was one of the great injustices of the world.

His father was clever.

But Matias was cleverer still, and he would see that he won this game.

His father wanted revenge for the loss of money.

Matias wanted revenge for the loss of his sister.

His motivation would always run deeper. It would always be more intense.

His motivation would always allow him to win.

Surely the monster couldn't win twice.

He stepped toward the dining room, and Augusta followed him. Then she went on through to the kitchen. "My staff has made coffee," he said.

"Excellent," she chirped.

Chirped.

She was far too cheerful about all of this. She returned with two cups of coffee, and set one in front of him, before taking a position down at the opposite end of the table and staring at him through the steam billowing up from her coffee mug.

"This relationship will be purely for show. No wedding. Just an engagement announcement."

"Agreed."

"I'm putting it in writing in the contract. There will be no sexual contact between us."

"*Tesoro*, surely you understand that there must be a level of physical contact between the two of us in public."

"A level. But remember, the fascination here will come from the fact that you're acting as a romantic and not a player."

"Your point?"

She lifted a shoulder. "What would people think if you looked at me differently. If you held onto me differently?"

"Why aren't you a publicist?"

"I don't want to be a wholesale minder of thoughtless billionaires."

"And yet you're so very good at it," he said dryly.

"I'm embroiled. I am at the center of this. Whether I want to be or not. That means I have to take some responsibility for it. I accept that. I intend to do that. I intend to come out of this like a damned Phoenix. I will rise from the ashes of your father. Not from yours."

She picked up her coffee mug, and took a sip.

"You are ruthless," he said.

"I can be. I don't come from anything. I

don't come from wealth or status. I come from a small town in Oregon. I never thought that I would see the world. I spent my life working to survive. Navigating complicated government systems and the flawed American medical system. I've been a caregiver. I'm not doing it again. What I do, I do for myself."

If he had been another man he might have asked for details. But he wasn't a man who knew people. He didn't need to know Augusta.

Still, it was impossible to ignore her fierceness here. Her conviction.

"All right. Romantic. I can do that."

He wouldn't sleep with her. Sex was what had gotten him into this situation, and he felt the need to reevaluate some things. That was the problem. He had committed to this one hundred percent. He gave no quarter. He had to become what the media saw in many ways. He didn't pause to reflect. Because the character that he played would never engage in self-reflection. But also because the predator within knew the steps.

He wondered how long it had been since he had engaged in any kind of reckoning.

Perhaps because the last one had been so painful, he had simply decided not to have them anymore.

Because breaking the connection between his heart and the world, his soul and himself, often seemed the most expedient way forward.

"I will require you to be available on demand."

"For a period of time," she said.

"Two months, and we reevaluate at that point."

"All right."

"But if I don't feel that the job is done, then the job is not done," he said.

"You must promise when all of this is done you'll speak highly of me. You'll make sure that my character is not besmirched, and you will recommend me, and my business to all of your billionaire friends."

He chuckled. "Done." He lifted a shoulder. "I am notorious for keeping things beyond cordial with women that I've associated with in the past. Thus ending our engagement will never reflect poorly on you."

"It can't reflect poorly on you either."

"No," he said. "If it does, then the whole thing will be for nothing."

"We'll evaluate that narrative at the end of the two months as well," she said. "We'll see how the wind is blowing in regard to the headlines."

"How soon can you collect your things from your hotel?"

"I only brought one bag."

"We are going to fly to London."

"London?"

"I think it's the best place for rampant media attention. It's either that, or New York or LA. I have offices in both places, but…"

"No. London."

"Perfect." She looked down at her hands. "I need to stop by Your Girl Friday before we make any public appearances."

"That is acceptable, but you will have to come to my penthouse no later than two o'clock in order to ready yourself for our public debut."

"That's fine. I can do that."

"Perfect. I will simply secure some new flight staff, and then we will be off."

CHAPTER FOUR

AUGGIE HADN'T FULLY thought through what he meant by securing new flight staff until they boarded the plane. Where she found herself being treated as Matias's guest, and not as the flight attendant. She knew a total out-of-body experience when she looked at a woman standing next to the liquor cabinet, wearing the same sort of smart outfit that Auggie normally did.

"Can I get you a drink?" the woman asked.

Auggie blinked. "Sure."

"Champagne," said Matias. "We are celebrating."

The woman, to her credit, did not ask *what* they were celebrating. Because of course people in her position knew that details would be revealed to them as the employers wished to reveal them.

It was the sort of thing that Auggie knew well.

Their champagne flutes were filled near to

the top, and she took a seat with him in the position usually occupied by his arm candy.

She grimaced internally. She didn't like to think of the women in reductive terms. Perhaps he was their arm candy. So there. Equality.

She took a sip of the champagne, which was undoubtedly the best quality she had ever had.

She was going to have to try and explain all of this to the work wives. She had a feeling that Irinka would be proud of the resourcefulness. That Lynna would be slightly wary, but overall see the merit of it. It would likely wound Maude's softer soul. For her part, Auggie didn't feel like she could afford to be a romantic. She had never messed around with men. She had too many important things to try and build. Too much to make up for. Too many experiences to reclaim, and relationships hadn't been high on the list, because they would come with an obligation to another person.

It just wasn't what she wanted. So this was… Strange, but it didn't mean anything to her as far as romance went.

As far as attraction went…

She knew exactly what he was. She had watched him engage in all manner of uninhibited behaviors.

She wasn't stupid enough to get herself involved in that.

He might not be quite who the media thought he was, but he was indiscriminate with his body.

And that was fine. His decision.

But she didn't need to go involving herself in it.

Auggie liked to be an expert before she jumped into anything.

And sexual contact with Matias would require expert-level skills.

She didn't even have entry-level skills.

So when they finished their champagne, and he extended his hand, drawing her out of her seat, his hands warm, and much rougher than she would've imagined, her heart leapt up into her throat. "Time for us to retire, I think." His eyes were intent on hers, and she could barely breathe.

It was hammering against her breastbone. But she followed him, into the bedroom. The one that she had just sneaked into so that she could make sure the woman he was with was not taking pictures of him.

He closed the door behind them and lounged on the bed.

"Nothing to do but wait for a while," he said.

She pressed herself against the door, her shoulder blades tight against the hard surface.

"I'm not going to molest you," he said. He rolled over onto his back and looked up at the ceiling. "I don't have any need of that."

"Oh, I'm aware," she said. "But this is slightly uncomfortable for me."

"Why?"

"I've been in here many times after you've finished entertaining yourself with your guests. Like I said, I check their phones. For nudes."

"You cannot tell me this has actually been an issue."

"How are you naïve? It's laughable. There have been many instances. I always come in and make sure that those photos are deleted. And they never realize it."

"You must be joking."

"No."

"I don't think anyone else ever did that."

"Maybe not. But there are pictures of you floating out around on the internet."

"I don't care about that."

"You don't care if your naked body ends up posted on the internet?"

"Do I strike you as someone with insecurities?"

"That doesn't mean you want the entire world to have access to…"

"Does that mean that you see me naked?"

"This is the kind of thing that I was worried about. Lines are being crossed."

"It's a genuine question," he said.

"Yes. Though, I can't say that I… Lingered on it."

"Then you have more restraint than some," he said.

"Nice to know that your ego is very healthy and undented in spite of everything that you've done to create the situation," she said.

"I didn't hire someone to break into my files."

"You also didn't protect them very well."

"Fair. I admit that I was complacent."

"I imagine it's difficult not to buy into your own press."

He frowned. "I don't think that I buy into my own press. I know how much of it's a lie."

"You know what everyone thinks about you. And I suppose it's easy to imagine that is true universally. That you are… This beloved playboy who is so enjoyed by women that of course one of them wouldn't actually be out to get you."

"I don't think that's the case."

"You don't think that's the case, but do you know any of the women that you slept with? Am I the first woman that you've ever conversed with in this room?" She wished that she wasn't like this. She wished that she didn't have to belabor the point. But she found that she did, even as the topic was making her uncomfortable. Even as she felt like she was breathless from talking to him about sex and his body in the enclosed space of this room.

She knew who she was. If she did choose to take a lover, it wasn't going to be him. Not one with so many strings attached. Not one who… Who created such powerful feelings inside of her. It was attraction, she knew that. And the worst thing was she knew that it was an incredibly basic response to him. It was simply how he made women feel. Because he was Matias Javier Hernandez Balcazar, and he was widely considered to be the most beautiful man in the world. It would be strange if she didn't respond to him in this way.

No. If she ever did decide to take a lover, it would be an English man, perhaps. And they would have a casual arrangement, where they met at a cottage on rainy afternoons, and they would drink tea and make love.

She did not think that Matias made love.

She rather thought that there was a rougher and cruder term for what he did in bed. And she ignored the tightening in her stomach that indicated she was interested in discovering for herself.

"No," he said. "But I don't actually talk to anyone. In fact, you and I have exchanged more honest conversation in the last few hours than I have with anyone in years." He didn't sound surprised by this, but a bit grim. And she felt…

How strange. How strange to know that this man had given more to her than he had to anyone else for a long time.

His connections were physical, theirs wasn't.

It made her feel…she couldn't parse it. She wasn't sure she wanted to.

"Anyone?"

"Anyone who knows me knows me on my own terms. And my terms are that I do not wish to be perceived."

"Why is that?"

"Because who I was doesn't serve me. At least not in any way beyond guiding me toward getting revenge on my father."

"You should tell me why you hate him."

"You've done research on me, I assume?"

"I know about you, yes. I've read your bio."

"Then you know I had a sister."

"Yes," she said slowly, "I know that you had a sister."

"What you don't know is that I'm responsible for her death."

He watched her process that information, her birdlike features knitted together tightly as she tried to take into consideration what he had just said. He didn't know why he wanted to push her like this. She was helping him. But perhaps what he really wanted to see was if she was up for this. Because it wasn't going to be easy. The truth was, Javier had set his sights on him. And that meant there would be more. So there could be no secrets between himself and Augusta, not really. He would have to make sure the same was true with her. Because things would come out. That was the truth of it.

His father would stop at nothing.

"You… You were responsible?"

"Yes. In order to explain, I will have to paint a clearer picture of how my father ran our household. My mother was meek and compliant. There was no other way to survive a life with him. He was cruel. He ruled with an iron fist. Though he never stooped to hitting us with it. He was an emotional manipulator, he would set a bar, and if we would clear it, he would tell us that we hadn't. He changed the metrics often. I wanted to please him. I bent over backward trying to make myself into the son that he wanted me to be. Seraphina... She kicked against it. She couldn't stand what he made of our mother. She couldn't stand being subjected to his demands. When she began rebelling, he did everything he could to stop it. He cut her off financially, he stopped our mother from speaking to her. I still kept in touch. It wasn't until later that I realized he allowed it for reasons of control. As long as there was a link between himself and Seraphina then he could still get to her. And as long as there was still someone she cared for in the family... There was something to exploit. I was... I was convinced that what he was doing was necessary. That Seraphina was harming herself, and... It wasn't wrong. Some of her behavior was self-destructive. And yet, his methods were not... It was not the way. But I didn't believe that, not at the time. At the time, I was a boy. I was his thing. His robotic soldier. I ordered the staff around the way that he did, I lived my life with ruthless precision. I denied myself all pleasures of the flesh. And when he told me that I had to go and give Seraphina the hard word that I would no longer be able to support her or be in her life unless she came home and complied with all of my father's demands… She overdosed. That same night. Because the one person she had thought cared about her had been acting as surveillance, had betrayed her in exactly the same way."

He had never told the story out loud before, and it sounded strange in his voice. He had said it in his own head many times. Cementing his culpability in what had happened.

He hated himself for it. He didn't hate himself less for hearing it said aloud. If anything, he hated himself slightly more, because it made him feel closer to the twenty-year-old that had done his father's bidding with such vigor. With such conviction.

"The most truly terrifying thing to learn about yourself is that you have the capacity to harm those you love, because you have been brainwashed. Manipulated. To realize that you are not half so clever as you think you are. That was when I decided that it all had to end. That was when… At Seraphina's funeral, when my father stood there without a tear on his cheek, I vowed that I would end him. But not only that, that I would prove the way he saw the world meant nothing. I decided to be all the things he had ever told me not to be, to compete with him, and to win. To destroy him. While smiling. You see, I have no desire to steal secrets from my father, I don't need them. But I do like to keep tabs on him."

"Matias... I'm sorry, I didn't know."

Her words were like a balm, but he refused to let it soothe anything.

"Why would you know? I've never spoken to anyone about it. It is immaterial. What happened then can't be changed. And that is the truly chilling thing about revenge plans, Augusta. They fixed nothing. They're simply more destruction in an already destroyed landscape."

"But if you feel that way, why do it?"

"Because I want scorched earth. I don't want to fix anything, I know it's impossible. I just want to salt the ground so that nothing can grow there ever again."

"Pitbull," she said. "I knew it."

"You said pitbulls weren't that aggressive."

"Mostly, they aren't. Like I said, they're reactionary. But when they're abused... They get mean."

"Apt, then," he said.

She seemed to be sitting with the revelation, though her next question wasn't about Seraphina. "Why let the media think you're... Simple?"

"Because I prefer to be unknowable. All evidence suggests that can't possibly be true, doesn't it? It's amusing, I think, that they see me as being something so utterly unthreatening."

"It allows you to move in the open," she said.

"Yes. Exactly. And in the end, I cannot imagine a more poetic headline. My father's fool of a son putting him out of business. Better that I'm not thought of as ruthless or brilliant or exacting. It makes my father's eventual downfall that much more humiliating for him."

"You thought of everything," she said.

"Absolutely everything," he repeated. "Except what I'll do when it's finished."

"Won't you just... Live?"

"Maybe," he said. But he didn't mean it.

The truth was, he was accomplished at numbing the pain. At blunting his grief with alcohol, with sex. He didn't touch drugs, because they had been the undoing of Seraphina, and he would never line the pockets of any of the people who had sold her illegal substances, he would never contribute to that trade. It had less to do with treating his own body like a temple of any kind and more to do with the festering rot of the industry.

"You can have a life, you know," she said.

"My sister doesn't," he said. "You can see where my dilemma is."

"Do you think that maybe it's not a great tribute to her to not live at all?"

"And what would you know about that?"

"I know about grief. Whether you can compare the two or not."

"Comparison is the thief of joy, I hear."

"My mother died," she said. "When I was eighteen. I never knew my father. She was the only parent that I had."

"I'm sorry. Let me tell you, a bad father is worse than no father."

"I suppose so," she said. "Neither of us would really know."

He nodded slowly. She had been alone in the world at eighteen. And she didn't seem to come from means. He wondered how she had navigated that. What she had done. He didn't ask.

It explained her. The determination, the scrap.

"We should land soon," she said. "Maybe I'll try to do some work."

"Is your computer in here?"

"Yes. I'll just… Sit over here."

And she did, at a desk in the corner of the room, working away, and he watched. Fascinated by her. By the focus that she gave to what she did. There was definitely more fire to her than he had ever seen when she was simply acting as his flight attendant. But she wasn't an entirely different person. She interested him more than he would like to admit. But he supposed that was a good thing. Because over the next couple of months they were going to spend a lot of time together.

CHAPTER FIVE

AUGGIE DIDN'T THINK she breathed properly until they landed in London, and she separated from Matias. She went as quickly as she could to the Your Girl Friday headquarters, in a lovely little office space in London. As soon as she arrived upstairs to their suite, she spread her hands wide and threw her arms up over her head. "I came up with a solution."

"Good," Irinka said. "Because I'm hearing rumblings through my contacts that the brewing storm is going to be a big one."

"I'm going to pretend to be engaged to him."

Everyone stared at her. Mouths open, eyes wide. Irinka did not look overly proud of her like she had predicted.

"You what?" Lynna asked.

"I decided that I would get a bigger boat. A bigger headline. And that headline is that notorious playboy Matias Javier Hernandez

Balcazar has traded in a life of debauchery for one of commitment."

"This is…not a good idea," Lynna said.

Auggie was instantly annoyed.

"Oh, are we going to talk about *bad ideas* now, Lynna? And what we all think they might be? Because we all agree that it is a bad idea you continue to go and stay at Athan Akakios' house once a year and *make him meals* when his father is responsible for the ruination of your entire family."

Lynna waved a hand like she was brushing Auggie's words out of the air. "You don't know what my eventual plans are. Perhaps I'm playing a long game. Death by Chocolate doesn't always have to be a metaphor, Auggie."

"If you're plotting murder on company time we do need to know about it, though," Maude said.

Maude could never stand for a creature to be in distress. But apparently beautiful Greek billionaires with dark souls were an exception.

Auggie couldn't argue.

But then, Maude turned her wide, compassionate eyes to Auggie.

"Let's not get derailed with Lynna. Why *you*?" Maude asked.

"Because, actually trying to find somebody who would do this, who could be trusted, fast enough... It is not even reasonable. I was there. I have to do it."

"In exchange for what?"

"Contacts. He is going to help grow our client base beyond our wildest dreams. I really do believe that."

"Do you?" Irinka said. "You really can't see what might go wrong with you pretending to get engaged to a client? It could open you up to all kinds of harassment. I am extra concerned with keeping boundaries in place."

She did know. Because Irinka's job was tricky, and it required total discretion. No one could know, broadly, that she did it, and yet the right people had to know when they needed her. But there could be no confusion among clients that she was an escort, either. Her lines had to be neatly and clearly drawn, while she stayed in the shadows and that was a difficult task.

Auggie never envied it.

"I know. I *know*," she said a second time just to make sure that she emphasized it appropriately. "I know exactly how loaded it is, and how big of a risk it is. Trust me. But either way, it's a sticky situation."

"We could just walk away," Lynna pointed out. "We don't have to be the cleanup crew."

"But if we are," Auggie said, "then imagine what that will do to our reputations. Imagine."

Everyone looked up, and it was clear that nobody wanted to endorse her acting as a sacrificial lamb in this way, but they could all absolutely see the benefit.

"I promise that I'll be safe. I'm drawing up an agreement." She went to the computer and sat down at her white desk. They had chosen to make their office bright, filled with light colors, golds and pastels. Because they were as tough as any man, but they didn't have to demonstrate that by sacrificing femininity. Far from it. Maybe that was her problem now. She was trying to right too many wrongs every time she did a single thing. They all were, honestly. The combination of the four of them, and all of their issues meant that they were a company comprised almost entirely of a desire to prove something. There were worse things. She really believed that. Far worse things.

But it made everything feel weighty. And just a little bit more intense at times.

She opened up a document, their boilerplate for a nondisclosure agreement, and then for terms and conditions of their association.

"You aren't going to sleep with him," Irinka said.

"No," Auggie responded, fighting the urge to laugh out of discomfort and a feeling of being caught. "Of course I'm not."

"Well, I just want to make sure you get that in the agreement."

She felt warm, and very uncomfortable. Like Irinka could see inside her head, inside to where all her secret fantasies were.

"Believe me, I've covered that. I know that you deal with a lot of men who try to push the boundaries of your agreement."

"Not anymore. My reputation precedes me. They know better."

"Good. I hope your reputation insulates me." The first thing she did was add in a clause that said no more physical contact than absolutely necessary, and only in public.

"You should put no contact below the waist. Or... In the front, above your waist."

"Are you telling me to put *Don't grope me in the Ts and Cs?*"

In spite of herself, her breasts felt heavy. He was not going to grope her. She didn't want him to anyway. It was actually laughable to think about Matias doing anything quite so prurient as that. Everything he did was sexual, yes, but there was nothing grasping or adolescent about it. She knew that all too well. She had watched the way his hand skimmed the curves of the women that he was with on the plane. Even while she had done her best to redirect her focus elsewhere. She had been aware.

It was impossible not to be.

She had done her best to try and block out the raw sexual nature that radiated from him, but of course that was extremely difficult.

She didn't like admitting that she was vulnerable to that part of him. Because it was pointless. She didn't want to be vulnerable to anything or anyone, frankly.

"You're snarling," Maude said.

"I am *not*," Auggie responded. She finished with the papers and sent them directly to his email. Then she slammed the laptop shut and stood up from the desk. "And do not tell me I look like a hedgehog, Maude. I'm good. Honestly, I just came to tell you all because it's going to break and it's going to break big. Tonight."

"That sounds so ominous. Like a prophecy from a fantasy novel," Maude said.

"It's not," she said. "Not even close. Thank you, though."

Their intercom buzzed. "Ms. Fremont, a car has arrived for you."

She frowned. Then she looked at her phone, and saw that she had a text from Matias. I need you to prepare yourself for tonight. Get in the car.

She scowled.

"Why are you scowling?" Maude asked.

"I'm scowling because he's already being annoying. But that's… That is the agreement I've made. To continue to deal with the Pitbull."

"Guard your chastity," Lynna said.

"Thanks, Lynna," said Auggie. "Do you happen to have a belt on hand?"

"No," she said, grinning benignly. "I've never needed one."

"I'll be safe," she said, scurrying back out of the office, and into the elevator.

She looked down at her phone. And then she sent back a text.

I hope this isn't going to be degrading.

When have I ever degraded anyone?

It was a good point.

I don't know. I'm not in your bedroom the entire time we are going on long-haul flights.

Very funny.

I am very funny, Matias.

I didn't know that about you.

You never really bothered to talk to me.

She had watched him be amusing, and witty. She had seen him be filled with a dark rage that made a sense of disquiet expand inside of her. But she had mostly been nothing to him. Nothing at all.

It was on purpose. How could it not be? But still, she realized that actually put her at a slight advantage. He didn't know her.

She pondered that all the way to the ground floor, and then when she exited the building she saw a stark black car parked against the curb.

She opened up the door and slipped inside, and shrieked when she slid down the seat, and against his hard body.

"I didn't know you would be in the car," she said, jumping back like an angry cat.

"Well, that's not going to be very convincing," he said.

"You startled me. There was a whole human in the car I wasn't expecting to see."

"I gather that."

She practically hissed and gathered herself into the corner of the car as it drove away from the curb.

"I have arranged for several stylists to come to my penthouse."

"Oh. Do you need a makeover?"

He treated her to a grin that was a bit more to see than the one he generally showed the public. "I'm fine the way that I am."

"Oh. So only the woman needs to be changed irrevocably to be acceptable. I thought you were supposed to be a progressive playboy."

"If by 'progressive' you mean that I love and respect women, then I suppose I am."

"Many people would argue that a man who is as promiscuous as you are doesn't respect women."

"That would only be true if you find sex inherently disrespectful. I believe that using another person for sex can be disrespectful. I believe that a man who acts as a selfish lover, who sees the woman that he's in bed with as less than him, or as someone worthy of contempt because she has chosen to sleep with him, is a man who ought to be hanged."

"Strong words," she said.

"It contributes to that great, unsolvable problem created in the world by men, does it not?"

"Explain," she said.

"Men want women to be sexually available. Yet judge them when they are. I have always found the standards of men to be unfair in that regard. And I have certainly never sought to perpetuate that sort of behavior."

"An activist."

"You said it, not me."

"Your father was that sort of man," she said, understanding then.

"Yes, he was. An exacting set of standards for others that he did not hold himself to. A hypocrite. I have no patience for hypocrites, Augusta. My sister was cruelly treated by a society that hates a rebellious woman. Who sees a spark of defiance in them is something to be crushed, not cultivated. What was a strength in me that could be reframed, was seen as a portent in her. I am a great many things, I have committed a number of sins in the pursuit of revenge against my father, and I have no doubt that I will commit innumerable sins more. But I don't hurt women. I do not hold myself to different standards than I would anyone else."

"And yet I'm the one getting the makeover," she said, though not quite so sharply as she might have, because the mention of his sister gouged her a bit.

"I already had mine. I think perhaps you don't understand exactly what I was back then. I might well have worn my suit as a military uniform. I was barely able to smile, let alone tell a joke. I could no more have amused a companion with a witty story than I could have pulled a rabbit out of the hat. I can do both, now, incidentally."

"Cheap magic tricks?"

"Sleight-of-hand can be useful for many things."

For some reason that made her face get hot. It should conjure up ridiculous images. Of Las Vegas and cheesy shows. But there was something about how he said it, how he looked at her when he did, that made it very clear he was talking about something else entirely.

Her body couldn't help but respond. She hated herself then a little bit. For being so... Susceptible to him. Even while he was saying exactly what he was. Maybe that was the secret. There was no shame in him, and he was exactly what he appeared to be. Every woman who got involved with him knew exactly what she was getting. It was well-publicized.

"Is that your secret?"

"What exactly?"

"You don't promise women anything. You are actually quite honest in some ways."

"In a sense," he said.

Of course, she also knew that he hid his intensity from everyone. She had seen it. It was a force. The kind that... That was the thing that could trap a woman. That intensity. When he played easy and affable, it was easy to believe that nothing else was there. That there was nothing deeper to him. That he was only the very shallow puddle he pretended to be, and that made it easy to think of him as a jungle gym that a woman could climb on and leave behind.

Not her, necessarily, but a woman. One who had experience of that kind of thing.

She had seen the intensity.

Just then, the car pulled up to his penthouse, delivering her from her thoughts. The building was beautiful, well appointed. She had been here before, but had never gone inside his residence. Just to the lobby. Which was all gold and marble elegance, ostentatious and fitting a jackdaw. A man who put brightly colored feathers over his plumage to disguise what he really was.

"You're the Scarlet Pimpernel," she said.

"Excuse me what?" he asked as he opened up the elevator that led to his floor.

"I was just thinking. You disguise your true nature behind a façade that allows people to underestimate you. It's a book. About a nobleman during the French Revolution who pretended to be an empty-headed fop in order to escape detection as a man who was helping people escape the gallows. It is also a movie, one that my mother liked quite a bit. So, I can pretend that I read the book, but I didn't."

"And you think that's me?"

"Yes. Essentially. It suits you to have people underestimate you, but only on your terms."

"Yes," he said, smiling wryly, "only on my terms."

They arrived at the top floor, and the elevator doors opened, revealing the grand scope of his penthouse. It was filled with people. She was trying to take in the opulent details of the room, but was distracted by the crowd that immediately rushed around her. "Jewel tones, I think," said one of the men. "Matching manicure," said a woman.

"I think perhaps a champagne-colored diamond."

She was being made over.

And she had no choice but to surrender.

CHAPTER SIX

MATIAS TOOK HIMSELF to his study while his team went to work on Augusta. She had looked deeply irritated with the whole thing, and he thought it best to let nature—by which he meant his well-paid team of experts—take its course.

He decided to make a phone call to his father.

"Hola," he said. *"Como estas?"*

"Is that you, Matias?" his father asked in Spanish.

"Si. I had wondered when we might connect again. What a shame it has to be under these conditions."

"The conditions that you have been stealing from my company?"

"A neatly fabricated fairy tale," Matias said.

"I do not think the information the whore sent to me is wrong."

Matias bit back a growl of rage. "No Father,

don't hire a woman to do a job and insult her because she did it well."

"Don't say I never gave you anything."

"Perhaps I cannot say that. But you took something from me. And I will never forgive it."

"If you are still upset about your sister, you must understand. There are people who are disposable. They will not amount to anything. Your sister might have lived ten more years, but the path she was on, she would've died young. On that you can trust me. Absolutely."

"You can say that about your own daughter?"

"I do not have a daughter."

Rage poured through Matias's veins. "I would never steal from you. Because you have nothing I value. Let us make that one thing exceptionally clear." It cost him then, not to make threats. Not to tell him exactly what he wanted to do to him. How what he really wanted was to wrap his hands around his father's neck and squeeze tight until the life left his eyes. No. Because he would be recording the conversation. Of course he would. He would want evidence that Matias was every bit as dark and damaged as he was accusing him of being. It was true.

"My life is going well," he said. "I'm on the cusp of a personal triumph. You can try to spread lies about me, but they will not prevail. How could they? I am well-liked, well-regarded, and more famous than you will ever be."

"You also behave as if you don't have a brain in your head. And people truly do love to uncover the sins of nepo babies these days, don't they? That is what they call it. What was once a legacy is now seen as an unfair advantage. And if they thought you steal directly from your father…"

"I think you'll find there are more interesting stories for them to read about this week." He paused for a moment. "I only want one thing from you, really, Father."

"And what is that?"

"When you get to hell, give me a call and let me know how hot it is."

Matias hung up the phone, not entirely satisfied with his discretion, but at least it hadn't been a literal threat. He considered that something of a triumph.

When he made his way back out into the living area, the flurry of activity was gone. It seemed as if they had all melted away now that their jobs were complete.

He stood there for a moment and looked around the ornate space. It was not to his taste at all. It was overly luxurious, overstuffed, over comfortable. It was made to be a haven for someone else. Someone who didn't exist.

He heard a door open, and he turned.

And there she was.

She was extraordinary.

Her glossy brown hair fell past her shoulders in sleek waves, a deep side part held fixed into place by a sparkling diamond flower. She was reminiscent of a Hollywood actress from the golden age. Her dress was strapless, her shoulders bare. The color a sort of electric orange that he would not have thought would be fetching on anyone, but was astonishing on her. Her matching lipstick and nail polish added to the effect. But it was the massive diamond ring on her left finger that truly drew the eye.

That was the point of all this. Not the way the dress shaped lovingly to a body that was curvier than he had realized, not the way her legs looked, elongated by the brightly colored pumps that she wore. No. The ring was the star of the show, and he could see it from across the room. A stunning display. That would call attention to itself instantly.

"Perfection," he said.

Her face shimmered, and while he was certain it had to be makeup, it seemed to come from deeper as well.

"And you say that I'm the Scarlet Pimpernel," he said.

It was like he had forgotten that anyone else was standing there.

"What does that mean?" she asked.

"Surely you must know what it means."

"I wouldn't have asked you if I knew," she said.

"Come," he said. "We will go downstairs and get in the car."

"Thank you," she said, turning around and facing the team. He did not bother to issue a thanks. They were well compensated.

"What happened to your famously good-natured demeanor?" She asked that question as soon as they were in the elevator. He could hardly recall having a good-natured demeanor.

"I just had a phone call with my father."

She blanched. "Oh. That doesn't seem like the best idea."

"Don't worry, I resisted the urge to transform into a mustache-twirling villain."

"Well, while that is good to know, it does

seem as if perhaps it was ill-advised timing on your part."

"I will see to my own timing, thank you."

He looked at her profile, at the gentle slope of her nose, the sharp curve of her cheekbone. She was an exceptionally beautiful woman, but beauty was a common thing. It didn't feel common just then.

Her beauty cut through the rage he felt now. The anger at his father. His anger at himself.

He was caught, just then, suspended between the reality of what he was, the role he played in the world, and the truth that was Auggie, and what she made him feel.

That she made him feel at all.

She challenged him. She unearthed parts of him long buried. He hadn't asked for that. He didn't want it.

She was silent for a moment. "But what did you mean by that? That *I* was the Scarlet Pimpernel."

It was her words that sliced through him. Cutting his normally impenetrable façade to ribbons. He wanted to return the favor.

"You have always seemed a perfectly pleasant looking woman, but you have a way of hiding yourself. You are more beautiful than any woman I've brought on the plane in your time there, and yet, you found a way to sort of blend into the background."

Her cheeks went red. "It's my job," she said. "Also, I am not *so* beautiful."

"How do you know that?"

"Because the only time a man has ever put a ring on my finger it has been for a ruse?"

"I've never been engaged either, and yet it is a truth universally acknowledged that I am extremely handsome."

"And very modest," she said, smiling up at him overly sweetly. Her complexion was clear, her brown eyes addictive. He wanted to keep searching for other layers of color in their depths. But that was a foolish thought. One perhaps that more matched a man who would've chosen that particular decor for his penthouse. And not who Matias truly was.

They got into the town car again, and were whisked to the trendiest part of the city where it was an absolute certainty that they would be seen and photographed. And that her ring would be noticed.

"We likely won't be set upon by paparazzi," he said. "Not until after this story breaks. This will be the calm. This will be the moment where we spark the imaginations of those around us."

"What is it like inside your head?" Augusta asked.

"What do you mean?"

"I have never thought that my mere presence would spark the imagination of anyone."

"And why not? You are stunning. Your mere presence could incite whole volumes of sonnets."

She looked away. "You're too good at that."

Was he? Was that what he was doing? His same old sort of display. He didn't think so. But then perhaps it didn't matter.

Perhaps all that mattered was that it had accomplished his goal. She looked happy. And they would look believably a couple. What else could he possibly want?

They arrived at the restaurant and when he opened the door, he reached out toward her. "It is time," he said.

She took his hand, and he pulled her out into the night. Into his world.

She had to remember not to get lost in this. Admittedly, she was kind of entranced by her own appearance. She had never looked like this. She had never looked so... Beautiful before. She had never really thought of herself as beautiful. She had thought of herself as someone who had an adequate canvas, she supposed. She knew how to fix herself up, though nothing like the way she had been fixed up today. She would never have chosen this color for herself, and yet it highlighted her pale complexion to perfection, it made her hair color seem deeper, more exotic—which was not what she would normally refer to the mousy brown as.

Indeed, nothing about her seemed mousy now. She was more than just Auggie from Oregon, who had lived a quiet life, learning to pay bills and manage medical visits before she had learned how to drive.

She felt… Special. She felt like she was sparkling. Nothing had ever been like this before, and it was tempting, so tempting, to let herself get lost in the fantasy.

To let herself get lost in him. Especially when he closed his large, firm hand around hers and pulled her out of the car.

His touch made her flutter. She couldn't deny that.

And then he looked at her and she… She melted. Inside.

She knew that it was a game. They'd just talked about how they both had the ability to hide themselves when they needed to. It should reinforce that this was fake and so were they, but it made her feel closer to him.

This man who was…only a day ago he'd been her boss. She'd watched him touch other women, but never her.

She'd never even let herself fantasize about it, and now here she was.

He was a force. It wasn't a mystery why women flocked to him, but there was something more in this moment. In being next to him and being so aware of the heat of his body, the masculine scent of him.

And how this had never been her before.

She was the one who took care of people. Who arranged things. Organized them. She was like a very accomplished stapler.

She didn't feel like a stapler, or wallpaper, or like a girl who had been stuck in her house for years taking care of her mother.

Right now, she felt like a woman.

That it was a game didn't change that. If anything, it *heightened* the way she felt.

So far away from the girl she'd been. A woman who was sophisticated enough to play games with the world's most renowned playboy.

She didn't feel like Auggie, not right now.

She was Matias's date.

He reached for her hand, and as his fingers wrapped around hers, her breath left her body in a gust.

She found herself relishing the feel of his touch. Rough hands, strong. His walk was sure and certain as he led her down the sidewalk to the restaurant. She looked to the left, and the right, she could see people taking photos of them with their cell phones. She didn't see any paparazzi, as he had said.

"If there are official photographers it will take them a while to arrive. Though I have deliberately taken us to a high-profile place. Where there are certain to be many celebrities out and about, which means there will be paparazzi."

Of course. It was a game, she knew that. In her sort of jack of all trades type of work, she had managed schedules, images and a great many other things. She didn't know how every sausage was made, but the fact was, she knew that the world was primarily comprised of complex sausage. It didn't just make itself. There were whole teams that were in charge of cultivating images, and making sure people were elevated in the right spaces and places. She just wasn't used to being the sausage.

That metaphor had run itself out. But she

was trying to distract herself. Trying to get a handle on her emotions. Because this wasn't real.

Anyway, she had never wanted this. She had never needed this kind of fantasy. It wasn't her. She didn't harbor secret dreams of being Cinderella. She didn't need that sort of thing.

Not even a little bit.

But it was a heady thing, feeling like she was part of this, even for a second. Having a man that looked like him on her arm. Yeah. It was a little bit more intoxicating than she would've imagined. She suddenly understood. Why women did this, even for a night. Nothing could've made her feel more beautiful than standing next to him, and she would've thought that it was quite the opposite. But no. To be seen as someone who was worthy of his attention… It was like a drug.

Powerful.

She hadn't realized that she was susceptible to such things. She truly hadn't.

But here she was, high on it and him. On feeling beautiful and shiny because she was in his orbit.

"You must endeavor to look happy," he said.

It was funny that she didn't look happy,

because she was actually enjoying herself. "I *am* happy," she said, looking up at him and smiling.

She knew that she had a very convincing smile, even when she was feeling other things. But she did feel happy now. It was just an enormous sort of happy that came with a weight, and an end point, and it made the happy feel weighted down. Sad at the same time as magical.

"You look very worried."

"I'm not. I'm only just... This is outside my experience."

"It won't be. Not in a couple of months."

Months. Two months of this.

"No." But it would be over then. Of course. That was the truth of it.

Her mouth filled with a metallic tang, and she chose to ignore it.

They walked up into the restaurant, and were ushered into a glorious, well-appointed corner. It was an old-style place, dark inside, rather than bright and modern like so many of the newer restaurants tended to be. It had a classic British menu, and she found herself charmed by it.

She found herself forgetting that they were on display.

What if she just pretended? What if just tonight she pretended that she was on a date with a beautiful man. What harm could it do? Anyway, it would allow her to be all that much more natural.

"I really never dreamed that I would travel the world," she said.

Sometimes it still shocked her to realize that she had. Sometimes she would count through all the countries she had been to— many of them since she had started working for the constantly in motion Matias—and she had to pinch herself.

"You didn't?"

"No. I'm from a small town. People don't really travel. I mean, sometimes they go to Disneyland, because it's not a very long drive. Only twelve hours."

"I forget how intrepid you Americans are with driving."

"The West Coast particularly is big. The states I mean. They're quite vast. So if you want to go to another state you have to drive."

"Like countries here."

"Yes. True."

"Where you from?"

"Oregon," she said.

She looked around. People were making

conversation in the restaurant, and there was music. No one would be able to hear exactly what they were saying. They simply looked like they were engaging in conversation.

"A place I have never been."

"You should go. It's beautiful." She thought maybe it was a little bit of a silly thing to say to a man with a private jet who could fly absolutely anywhere. But she did stand by that. She had been to so many places now, and she still thought her home state was one of the most beautiful places she had ever been to. Someday, she would probably go back and live there. Someday.

It would be different to live there if she wasn't stuck.

"It is cold there, isn't it?"

"Not as cold as some places in the US. And if you're thinking of all the rain, you're thinking of the northern part of the state. It actually gets very hot where I'm from."

"That would work for me," he said. "I'm used to Spain and I did a significant amount of business in London."

"Do you prefer London to Spain?"

"You would have to be a fool not to prefer Spain. In my opinion."

"You don't spend a ton of time there."

"I have memories there that are far too complicated."

She nodded. "I understand that. I mean… I remember feeling trapped. Trapped in a small town. Trapped in my life. I didn't think it would ever change. I didn't think I would ever go anywhere."

"And what changed?"

"My mother died." Unexpectedly her eyes filled with tears. It had been so long. It didn't usually hit her like that. And yet, it was always so complicated. So many layers. Her own trauma, her own pain. Her own sadness. Her own gratitude. She was swamped by all of it then.

"Did your mother not want you to travel?"

"Someone had to take care of her. She was terminally ill for most of my childhood. And… We had to make it seem like we had it all together, otherwise Child Services would've gotten involved, and I didn't want that. But you know, she was a single mother. A little bit older. I had to make sure that she was able to get to her fusion appointments, and she took her medication. I had to help her manage the symptoms of both her illness and her treatment."

"How did you go to school?"

"I finished at home. I… I didn't mind it. I didn't. She was my mother, I loved her very much. There was a time where I couldn't see past it either. And the truth is, when you start to wish away the burden that comes with care like that, you realize that you're wishing the person away too. And that is a horrible feeling. One that I… I never really wanted to contemplate."

"I'm sorry for your loss," he said.

And she thought maybe he even meant it. She had told him already that her mother had died, but not about this.

"I learned to be organized, meticulous. I learned to look like I had everything together even if I didn't. I learned to smile. It actually set me up for my job. Better than school ever did. And when she died I had a bit of money, and I used it. I sold the house, all the things. There was some insurance, and I went to school, met my work wives, and we decided that an adventure in London would be the way to go. Connect us with the world a bit more."

"Work wives?"

"That is what I call them. Irinka, Maude and Lynna. They really are about the only family I have."

She knew that it was a performance, she wasn't foolish. She knew that this was the kind of thing that he did every day of the week, and even though there was some more heft to this performance than usual, it was just a regular Saturday night for him. For her it was something singular. She understood why they did it, in that moment. All these women that had fallen to his charms, she understood it. Because this was intoxicating. He knew exactly how to make you feel like you were the center of attention. Like there was no one else in the world and never had been. She felt beautiful, in a way that she never had. And perhaps, most outrageously, most unfairly, she felt like she was the center of everything.

This beautiful man looked at her as if he had nothing else to look at.

She hadn't even realized that she craved this until this moment. Until she felt the intense magnetic pull of his gaze.

What would it be like to surrender and have one beautiful night with him?

"You really shouldn't look at me that way," he said.

"Like what?" She felt breathless. She knew that she was tempting something by asking him that question. She knew it.

"Like you're considering violating the terms of the agreement."

"Neither of us have signed anything yet."

"That is true. There is still time to revise."

He was a shameless flirt. It was confusing, though, because she had seen just a little bit of the real him. Because she had seen beneath the façade. So why bother now? Was it simply because he didn't know another way to be? Or maybe… Well, he was a man. She supposed it was possible that his sex drive was simply that healthy. Yes. That was definitely possible.

"I don't know about that," she said.

Irinka had warned her. About how people would see her. About what clients would think. And she understood something brilliantly true in that moment. It didn't matter whether she slept with him or not. People would think that she had.

And so, was it so outrageous to consider the possibility of getting something out of that?

She was a virgin. Not because of any strict morality on her part. Not because she was waiting for somebody. Because she had never been swept off her feet. Because nobody had ever inspired her to do something, to want something, other than what she had.

The idea of a lover felt like an interruption. But Matias Balcazar had crashed into her life like a freight train. They were trapped together. And if they were going to be the toast of the town, the delights of London, New York and every other city, why shouldn't she know what it was to have his hands on her body, his mouth on her neck? She had seen him kiss other women, touch other women.

She had also seen the way that he looked at those women. He thought she was beautiful.

But if he just feels the same about you as he does everyone else, is it really special?

You don't need it to be special.

No. Of course she didn't. Why should she have a need to be special? Special was... It wasn't important. Special didn't signify. Not if this was just a ruse. Something to help them pass the time.

"You've probably never been celibate before," she said.

He chuckled. "You don't think that I was a late bloomer?"

"Somehow no."

"You would be wrong." His dark eyes searched the vicinity of the table, as if he was making sure no one was eavesdropping. "I was my father's minion, remember. My behavior was above reproach. Until it wasn't. I stayed away from the pleasures of the flesh until I was twenty."

That was like a small hand grenade thrown into the center of the table. She had imagined he'd been a libertine his entire life. Yet, she'd known that there were parts of him that didn't match his exterior and this gave her a window into that which almost felt…wrong to have. Illicit in a way.

It made her mouth dry. It shouldn't.

It was just the subject of sex. When she wanted him, no matter how she tried to pretend she didn't.

The subject of virginity when she knew full well the status of her own.

"Wow," she said. "I would never ever have guessed that you were a virgin until you were twenty." She shifted in her seat, being a virgin at the ripe old age of twenty-five and feeling quite rude for calling him out for holding on to his virginity for a mere two decades.

"Twenty-one," he said. "I didn't immediately jump into bed with a woman in the throes of my grief."

"And you spent all the years after making up for lost time?"

"I don't know that I would put it that way. What I did, I suppose, is decide to be different. In every way. From what I had been before. From what my father had tried to make me."

His eyes were dark and sharp, and they collided with hers. She felt something grow taut in her stomach, at the same time her limbs began to loosen.

She wanted him. It was outrageous. They were sitting here talking about their lives. Having a fake date that felt more real by the moment.

She shouldn't be thinking about sex. It was a performance. But she wanted this man. This man whose father had wounded him so deeply it had scarred him forever. This man who had fashioned himself into a libertine as a form of revenge, not because it was who he was.

This man who, she had known from the beginning wasn't what he seemed, because she had just…known.

Because she knew what it was like to have the potential for who you could have been stolen from you by life, by tragedy. Even when it wasn't something another person did to you on purpose, she knew.

She could never know who she would have been if she hadn't had a sick mother.

She could never know what she might have

done if she'd been born into a happy, carefree life. Maybe she wouldn't be here. Maybe she wouldn't be a virgin at twenty-five.

But she was. And she was here.

She'd said she wouldn't sleep with him. She'd promised her friends.

She wanted to break her promises. Because for a moment she just wanted to be Auggie. Stripped down to her deepest, most basic needs. And she wanted to have those needs satisfied.

She had stopped being careful around him that day in Barcelona. She wasn't going to be careful now.

She was going to ask for what she wanted.

"Do you want me?" She had to know the answer to that question.

His dark eyes flickered over her. "You're very beautiful."

"You've been with a lot of beautiful women. Beautiful women that I've seen. More beautiful than me. So if that's the only thing that matters…"

"You fascinate me," he said. "And that is the very reason that I should tell you I don't want you. I cannot afford fascination. Nor do I want it. I don't need a woman to be special. I treat her like she's special, and in that moment she becomes my world. But when I decide that she is no longer my world, I walk away. I create the intrigue. I do not succumb to it. You intrigue me. Without my permission. And I'm not quite sure what to do with that."

She loved that. That she was destroying his shields in the same way he did hers. That she wasn't alone in this.

A heady rush of need filled Auggie. She wanted to be the focus of that. For just an evening.

She looked down. "I've never been with anyone. I spent all those years taking care of my mother, and then... Then I just tried to get away. I tried to put as much space between myself and the old world as I could. I tried to be somebody different. I... I never stopped. I never wanted to take care of anyone ever again. Just myself. And so I have. But it's a very lonely sort of existence. Sometimes I... Okay, that's a lie. I was going to say sometimes I want to connect with someone. I don't. I never have. I have my friends, and that's been enough. Right now I'm wondering. I'm wondering if I want more. If I need more."

"Are you propositioning me?"

"They're going to call me a slut. I might as well be one. If I can't control the way that people are going to see me when all of this is over, then perhaps I should get something for my trouble."

"You've never been with anyone?" His dark eyes were alight with a terrible fire that excited her, that thrilled her down to the soles of her feet.

"No one."

"You realize that's a rare and precious thing to offer to a man like me. I don't traffic in the rare and precious. I am very good at what I do."

"What is it you do?" She leaned in, tenting her fingers, resting her chin on top of them.

"Little girl, don't push me."

"Tell me," she said, the tension inside of her rising up to unbearable levels. The temptation to throw everything away, everything but this, everything but her need.

"This seems very out of character for you," he said.

"It is. But all of this is. It's an incredibly foolish thing. But I've never played with fire before, and I'm sort of enjoying the idea of it."

"What I do, is I give women pleasure. But then I forget about them. And you must never lose sight of that. At the end of this time together, I will never think of you again. I can't anymore."

"I know that you're not a silly playboy who doesn't feel anything."

He took a breath. "I'm worse than that. I'm a monster who puts on a playboy smile, and charms everyone around him. But I feel very little."

She didn't think that was true. She'd seen him shimmering with dark emotion on more than one occasion. She thought he felt too much.

He would never admit it, though. But she knew it all the same.

She didn't know where her boldness came from. She got up from her seat, and moved to the one next to him, her heart pounding heavily. "Do you feel pleasure?" she asked, her mouth inching ever closer to his.

"Auggie," he said. The first time that he had ever said her name out loud like that. August, that was what he normally called her. And she didn't mind it, but hearing him say her nickname did things to her.

"What?"

"I'm attempting to warn you off. I've never carried on a two-month affair with anyone in my life."

"It doesn't need to be two months."

"We are going to be in each other's vicinity, and you honestly think that if we sleep together, once will be enough?"

"Maybe it will be. I don't care about the future. And all I have ever cared about is the future. But I want… What I want is this fantasy. This one. Where we are both beautiful, and nothing else matters."

There was a look in his eye in that moment that she couldn't quite define. A desperation. Like he wanted to claim that for himself as well. Like he wanted to believe in the façade too.

"Why can't we?"

"All right," he said. "My beautiful fiancée."

It sent a shiver down her spine. This wasn't her. It was a character she was playing. But it was glorious all the same. She loved it. This was the sort of dangerous game she would never allow herself to play under any other circumstances. This was the luxury of touch, of being desired, being wanted that she had always denied herself, because she never wanted to be needed, not ever again. Not emotionally. She could be needed at her job, but it was different.

But this was only a game. He couldn't feel anything, couldn't want anything from her.

And all she could want from him was this.

Her friends would be appalled. But they would understand. They all worked so hard. They all had their own issues, their own demons. Their own hang-ups when it came to men. Surely they wouldn't resent her trying to reclaim some of what had been lost to her.

"Take me," she said.

"I will. Don't you worry."

CHAPTER SEVEN

THIS WAS A very bad idea, and he knew it. But he was gripped with need. He didn't want her to know what a terribly rare thing this was. Yes, he enjoyed sex, he enjoyed women. He was not the sort of man to allow himself to be taken in like this. He did the seducing, not the other way around. And having a woman, a virgin, affect him in this way was...

It was...

He knew he shouldn't want it. He knew he shouldn't want her purity. That he shouldn't want to be the first person to ever touch her, to ever take her, to ever show her what pleasure meant.

She had captivated him from the first moment he'd seen her. And then again at his house, and again when she'd had this makeover. And it was something other than beauty.

He just... He just wanted her. After the conversation with his father today, he wanted something to distract him, but not in the same sort of way he often craved mindless desire.

It was something new. Something different. And for a man like him novelty was an art.

A rare gift, and he intended to seize it. Intended to have this moment out of time.

As if you deserve it.

Everything felt raw and close to the surface, but that made him want this even more. He had a feeling that she saw him. More the real him than most women did. Than most anybody did.

And yet she still wanted him. Perhaps, she even wanted him because of it, and there was something about that that drove him now.

They left the restaurant, hand in hand, they didn't stay out as long as they should have. The entire point of this was to put on a show. But he found himself growing impatient. He took her hand and led her to the car. And once they were inside, he gripped her face, forcing her to stare into his eyes. "What is it you want from me?"

"Nothing," she said breathless. "Nothing more than you."

"And what do you see when you look at me?"

She searched his gaze.

"A beautiful man. But a troubled one."

"Not wrong. And you want me anyway?"

"I find you fascinating."

"Why?"

"I don't know," she said. She was being honest, he could tell.

"Maybe you just waited to have sex too long, and you think that I'll make it good."

"Yes. But that's not... No offense, but there are many good-looking men. I went to college with quite a few."

"As good-looking as I am?"

"Maybe not," she said, shaking her head. "But if all I was after was a handsome man, I wouldn't be a twenty-five-year-old virgin."

"So tell me that. You're a virgin. You steadfastly refused to have sex with me just earlier today. Why now?"

"Because you made me feel special. And I don't care if it's real or not. I don't care if it's true. That's why I need it to be tonight, in fact. Because I want to stay in this dream. I want to be the person that's seen. Do you understand? That has never been me. That's never been my life. I am the wallpaper, Matias. Always and ever. I am the woman who blends in, the woman that serves drinks, the woman who assists. The child that brings medication, and makes doctor appointments, but I am never wholly myself. Or special. Or wanted. And you make me feel like I could be. I just want that. For a while."

He wanted the same, he realized. Because she looked at him and saw someone who might treat her right. Might give her something real, something good, and he wanted to be that fantasy for a while. More than just a fantasy of good sex, more than just seduction. He wanted to have the same fantasy she was having. Because maybe, just maybe, they were both special in that world. Maybe she mattered and he wasn't beyond redemption. Just maybe.

Then, he could hold back no longer. He closed the distance between them, bringing his mouth down hard on hers. She whimpered. And froze. He could feel that she wasn't an expert, but she was soft, and she tasted like magic.

Sex had long ago lost any sort of magic. He enjoyed it. But it didn't feel like this. It never had. He could remember his first time, which he had gone about grimly. Because it was time. Because he was trying to strip off the last vestiges of what he had been. Of who he had been.

Because he was trying to learn to be the playboy. Sex for him had been a series of scourings. Of stripping back layer after layer of who he had once been, to make something new beneath it.

But this didn't feel that way. This felt like something singular. Something real.

He could not quite fathom it.

So he kissed her. He poured everything into that kiss. All the need, all the darkness that he suspected she saw. She gasped, and he took the opportunity to take the kiss deeper, to slide his tongue against hers, and make her his.

He kissed her. Again and again.

He wanted her. He wanted this.

"I am going to take you," he said. "Just as you demanded. But you must be very certain that it's what you want. Because you're right, I don't degrade women. Unless they ask."

Her cheeks were bright and flushed, her eyes glittering. "I don't even know what to ask for."

"Then I shouldn't have you. I shouldn't have anyone so innocent that she doesn't even know what she wants."

"Everyone has to start somewhere, don't they?"

Maybe that was the magic. That she was asking him to help be the one to reform her. To shape her sexuality. To make her his. Maybe that was it.

Because for all the experience his jaded palate had tasted, this was unique.

He had never experienced this.

Not ever.

Maybe it was the novelty.

And it would wear off. But not tonight.

"Will your friends be consumed with worry if you don't contact them?"

"I'm a grown woman. I can take care of myself."

"Some would say that you're perhaps doing a very bad job of it right now."

"Maybe," she said. "But some would say that I'm doing a very good job."

He chuckled. "A good point."

"After all, you have to think that sex was inherently dangerous to think that I was putting myself at risk." He rubbed his thumb over her cheekbone. "The way that I do it can be quite dangerous."

"I need you to show me. Otherwise I'm going to be convinced that you're all talk." She was so bold. She always had been. But then, he imagined that she would have to be.

To build this business out of nothing. To take the sorts of chances that she and her friends had when they were so young. When she had come from nothing. It was easy to believe that it wasn't a skill to stand in the background. Easy to convince oneself that it was the wealthy who had succeeded through their cunning and prowess, but this woman came from nothing, and had created from that so much.

Of course she was brilliant. Singular. And very, very brave.

"You don't fear much, do you?" he asked, his voice hoarse.

"No, not much," she said.

But she was afraid of things. Of course she was, everyone was.

But there was no room for that now. And thank God.

Because he just wanted her.

So he kissed her again, until the car came up against the curb. Until it was time for them to get out, and headed to the building. But he did not take his hands off of her. He found he didn't want to. Dimly he was aware that they had been followed. The photographs were taken. All the better. Because people might cry PR relationship, no matter what they did, but if they saw them together like this, clearly about to go upstairs and engage in intimacy, then it would be much harder for them to convince the world of it.

There would be headlines tomorrow. A cascade of them. He knew that. But tonight there was just them.

That was all.

They were in a cocoon of passion, and he allowed that to propel them to the elevator, up to the top floor. And into that lavish penthouse. Where he was suddenly grateful that it was a playboy's haven, because every surface was soft for a reason.

He took her into his arms and he kissed her. "I will show you," he said. "Everything you like." He kissed her neck, and he began to unzip her dress as he traveled down her body, kissing the curve of her breast as he separated the fabric away from her curves. As he stripped her down to brief, lacy underwear, and her red high heels.

"Beautiful," he growled.

Her eyes were round, and he could see a hint of nerves, but she was doing her best to hide them, and he thought that he would honor that.

A virgin.

Of all the things.

There were gifts that no man could ever possibly deserve. This was one of them. To be the first man to touch her beautiful body? Outrageous.

He was worth very little. He had failed the one person that had ever loved him. That had ever needed him. Surely that meant he shouldn't have nice moments like this one.

You are outside of time and space. Let her take you away.

That was a first. Sex, to him, was an opportunity to remove himself from everything he had been raised to be, one encounter at a time. He took pride in pleasuring women, and honoring them with the act, but he did not feel as if he was escaping. Did not feel as if he was getting something out of it.

But tonight, he did. Tonight he was claiming it for himself just as much as he was claiming it for her, whether he deserved it or not.

He licked the plump curve of her breast, and then undid her bra, exposing her generous breasts to his gaze. He was starving for her. So he fastened his lips to one raspberry nipple, sucking it in deep. She arched her back and gasped, forking her fingers through his hair. He loved her boldness. That she wasn't bothering with protests, and virginal proclamations of embarrassment. But then, how was he to know if virgins actually did those things. He had never been with one before.

Plus, he couldn't speak to the nature of her fantasy life. Or to the amount of other experience she had with men. She arched against him, and he pressed her firmly against the wall, before kissing down her body and tugging her underwear down her thighs. He parted her legs and began to lick her deeply. She gasped, moving in time with the rhythm of his mouth, his lips, his tongue.

She tasted like the dessert that they had left before they could have.

She tasted like a dream.

And he was getting as much as he was giving in this moment, if not more, he was on edge. Fulfilled and undone by the taste of her.

He licked her, deeper and deeper and she cried out, on the verge of a climax. So he decided to push her there. He pushed one finger inside of her as he continued to lick her, and he felt her unravel, felt her internal muscles clenched around him. Then he moved back up to her mouth and kissed her deep. "Let's go into the bedroom."

She nodded wordlessly. And then, naked except for the high heels, she began to walk toward his room.

She didn't know herself. But she didn't want to.

She didn't want him to say her name, not again, even though it had thrilled her slightly to hear it earlier. Because she didn't want to think of herself as Auggie Fremont right now. She wanted to be out of space and out of time. She wanted to be someone different than she had ever been before.

She wanted to be somebody new.

She wanted to weep because she didn't feel like her. She felt like something more special. Brighter, better.

She felt exquisite. And it was because of him.

The orgasm that he had just given her had rocked her, shaking her. It was so much different than pleasuring herself. She had no control over it. He had called it from her body like he was the master of her pleasure. And she wanted to surrender. So when he ordered her to go into his room, she obeyed.

"Wait for me on the bed," he said.

She did, her heart hammering.

He stripped off his suit jacket, his tie, his shirt. She had seen him half-naked a hundred times. But nothing prepared her for being on the receiving end of the intense look in his eye as he removed his clothing. Realizing that body was for her. That his touch was for her.

She was overcome with it.

She watched as his muscles rippled, his golden-brown skin making her mouth water. The dark hair that covered his muscles made her fingertips itch. She wanted to touch him. She wanted to lick him. It was like a dam had burst inside of her, and every desire that she had held back for all this time was ready to burst forth.

She had tried so hard to be good. Maybe she wasn't good. She was okay with that.

Tonight, she was okay with it.

He moved his hands to his belt buckle, to the closure on his slacks, and he stripped off the rest of his suit, and right then, she understood something dark and terrible. Looking at the full power of his rampant masculinity, she knew something, a deep, real truth that had always been hidden from her before.

This was an addiction. This was why countries fell to ruin. It was why good women craved very bad men. It was why good men broke apart families. This was something more powerful than she had fully given it credit for. And she wondered if she was horrendously naïve to believe that it was something that she could shut off after tonight.

It doesn't matter. Because tomorrow is going to take care of itself.

Yes. It was.

So she surrendered to his beauty. To her need. To his touch, when he made his way to the bed and moved himself over the top of her. She kissed his neck. Kissed her way down his chest, his ridged abdomen. She moved to that sick, glorious masculine part of him, and took him into her mouth. She wasn't nervous. She wasn't anything except filled with the most alarming, terrible, painful need.

She took him in deep, pushing her own limits. She reveled in the fact that she could make him groan. That she could affect him at all.

And maybe it was because he was a man. And men were that simple. But maybe it was because she was a woman, and she was that powerful. She was going to remember that.

From this moment onward.

She licked him, because she couldn't help it. Luxuriated in the taste of him, in the feel of him beneath her tongue.

Until he gripped her hair and pulled her back up his body and claimed her mouth in a furious kiss. "Now," he growled, opening up the nightstand next to the bed and taking out a box of condoms. He took out one plastic packet, tore it open and rolled it over his thick length. She gave thanks for his speed and efficiency. He moved between her legs, but before he penetrated her, he pushed one finger inside of her, then another. "So wet," he ground out, and his appreciation sent a spark of need shimmering through her, threatening to set off an explosion. "This may hurt," he said.

"That's okay," she said.

He withdrew his fingers, and moved back to her, kissing her mouth. Then he tested the entrance to her body with the head of his manhood, pushing in inch by glorious inch. It did hurt. But she didn't mind.

It was wonderful. To be filled by him, possessed by him. Claimed by him.

She arched her back, and cried out as he filled her to the hilt. As he took her. Just as she had demanded.

This was everything. And so was he.

He began to move, the spell he was casting over her finding her in its dark magic. Binding her to him. The pleasure that built inside of her was deeper than the pleasure from before. The climax coming from somewhere at her very center.

And as she cried out his name, she lost herself completely. But the real triumph was when he let go. When he shivered with need, pulsing deep within her, his own control lost at the threshold of desire.

She clung to him.

Matias.

Perhaps she whispered his name. Perhaps it was only an echo in her soul. She didn't know.

But for tonight, it was perfect. Tonight, everything was wonderful.

Tomorrow would take care of itself.

CHAPTER EIGHT

IT WAS FIVE THIRTY when his phone buzzed.

"You will regret trying me."

His father's voice, angry and acrid, came down the line, but before Matias could respond, he was gone.

Matias sat up. Auggie was lying in bed beside him, the sheets pushed down to her waist, her arm thrown up over her head. She looked like a marble statue in motion, her breasts on display, her beauty arresting. But he could not focus on her beauty. Not just now.

He got out of bed and pulled on his pants.

"Where are you going?" Auggie asked, her voice sleepy.

"I just have to…"

The next phone call was from his publicist. "About time you got in the game," he snarled.

"We have a much bigger problem than we anticipated."

"What is the problem?" He asked the other woman.

"Your father has decided to drag everything out into the open."

Well. Not everything. Matias knew that without even checking. Because the truth would only paint him in a bad light. But what he had decided to reveal...

His phone buzzed, and he looked at his text from his publicist. At the headline there.

Matias Balcazar Accused of Corporate Espionage Against His Father, Causing his Sister's Death!

"Bastard," he said.

"What statement would you like me to make?"

"Isn't my job to figure out what statement you should make. It is yours. Do it." He hung the phone up.

He turned around and saw Auggie standing there with her sheet pulled up around her body, her hair in disarray. "What's wrong?"

"This is... This has escalated."

Auggie moved across the room and ran for her purse. It was obvious that she already had a raft of texts. "Oh, no," she said.

"Yes," he said, his voice hard. "Oh, no, indeed."

"You're not responsible for her death."

"I am," he said. "I am. I delivered the exact message that my father told me to give her. And I told her that with the shame she was bringing on the family would be better off without her."

"Matias…"

"What was she to assume except that she would be better off dead?"

"A lot of people have issues with their family and they don't overdose."

"But she did. She did, because she was fragile. Because she needed me to be her ally, and I was not."

"You can't take responsibility for all of it."

He turned, fury in his veins like fire. "Yes. I can. And my father is demanding that I do. This is what he's doing. To eclipse our attempts at controlling this. Come with me."

"Where are we going?"

"We need to get out of the city. We need to rethink things."

His heart was pounding harder than it should. He felt like he was perhaps about to have a heart attack.

"What happened?"

"He's putting out everything about my sister. Everything. And my involvement in her death."

She shook her head. "But you didn't kill her. You weren't responsible for her death."

"I was," he said. "Believe me, I was. And it is all being put out there in black and white, and anyone who reads it would think the same."

"If you are responsible, then so is your father."

"But it doesn't matter to him. It doesn't matter. It matters to me. That he would... This is sacred ground to me."

"I'm sorry," she said.

She looked small, hurt. He imagined that what she was hoping for was better treatment the morning after she had her first sexual experience, but he couldn't afford to think about that right now. He couldn't afford to let it matter.

She had seen him make a mistake with Charmaine. And now this.

He growled, moving into his bedroom and beginning to dress as quickly as possible. She blinked, and he noticed that her eyes were full of tears.

"I don't have anything to change into."

"It doesn't matter. If you're seen leaving my house in the same thing that you wore inside, it only lends itself to the illusion."

"Do you honestly think that it matters now?"

"I'm sure that it's in the news somewhere. Buried beneath this."

"Then I will make a show of standing beside you. Whatever you need." She would make a show of it. Because of course it was a show. For a moment, last night, it had felt like perhaps she knew him. Much in the same way it felt like he might know her. It had felt like something different. Something real. Something that he had never experienced before. But it had been a game. All of this was a game. Every moment of every day that he had breathed since Seraphina had died had been a game, and forgetting that had been his first mistake. You could not escape your past. You couldn't escape the darkness there.

She left, her clothes in her arms, and returned moments later, dressed in the same clothing from the night before. The color that had seemed so suitable to her last night seemed somewhat garish today. In the bright light of the morning, clearly announcing that he had debauched her, that he was using her.

That's what he was doing. That's what he had been doing to every woman that he had ever met since he had embarked on this.

How he had thought that he had escaped bad behavior simply because he was a good lover, because he considered himself respectful, he didn't know.

It was all a game.

He might not have chosen to play it. He was.

And in the end, when the headlines were released, the truth was he was no different than his father.

He was a man who had his own way of doing things and did it regardless of the impact on others. A man who behaved in supremely selfish ways, and treated those around him as if they were pawns in a game, rather than human beings.

But this was not even the time for self-pity. Because this was a mess of his own making, and he would do what needed doing to clean it up. Because it wasn't only what had been written about him, but what was being written about Seraphina. The way that it seemed to indicate that he didn't care about her. "We need to get down to my office."

"All right," she said.

"I suppose you want to call your friends."

"It can wait."

They headed down the street, and this time, when he called for a car, he did not ask for a driver. But as his car was brought into place for him by the valet, he noticed that there were paparazzi. Everywhere. Lining the streets, their black SUVs a telltale sign.

"Quickly," he said.

They got behind the wheel and he began to drive, maneuvering out of the city.

"Where are you taking us?" she asked as they crossed the first bridge.

"I have a house. In the country. If we make it there, then the paparazzi will not follow us. I'm certain that once we leave the urban sprawl, they'll give up."

"I thought that you had to get back to your company."

"It would be a good idea, but do you not see…" He looked in the rearview mirror. "There's an entire cavalcade."

She looked, worried. And then she began to text.

"Your work wives?"

"Yes. I'm asking them for some help."

"See if they can create a diversion."

"I will."

But the car was gaining on them, and there was a photographer hanging out the window, taking his picture.

It sent panic through him. He couldn't quite say why. Because Seraphina was dead, so what did any of this matter? Except it was him. He disliked seeing all of this in black and white so intensely because it highlighted his culpability in all of it. And if he was going to take his father down, perhaps he should take himself down with him. Perhaps... Perhaps there was nothing about him that was worth much of anything at all.

Perhaps he deserved to be gone as well.

But it was better, yes, it was better, and perhaps it was for him, to go through life as an avenging angel. To act as if his mission to destroy Javier would atone for something. How could it?

A few of the cars abandoned them as they continued on down the winding roads, as he began to drive faster.

"Be careful," she said, hanging onto the door handle.

"I'm being careful," he said.

But then, they came to a crossroads, and a dark SUV pulled out quickly in front of them. He swerved, and the car went off the road, and when he realized that the passenger side was about to connect with the tree, he corrected sharply, hitting the front end, the airbags failing to deploy, his head making a cracking impact against the steering wheel. His face was throbbing, and he felt warm blood running down his cheekbones.

"Matias…" Her voice was distant.

"I'm fine," he said, seeing if the engine would start. It did. He threw his car into reverse, and drove even faster down the road, blood spilling into his eyes. His vision blurred, but he kept on driving. At least the paparazzi were no longer in pursuit. He pulled off quickly to a hidden road, and then the other, which would take him to his gated estate here in the country. He entered the code, and started to drive up the road and toward the house. It was several kilometers off of the main road, and they would not be disturbed there. It was nearly impossible to get inside.

"Matias."

For the first time, he glanced over at Auggie. She looked terrified, pale. There was a large bruise forming on her cheek.

"Are you hurt?"

"I'm not great. Why didn't the airbags deploy?"

"I don't know. And I will buy the manufac-
turer and put them out of business."

"I don't know that that's necessary."

"You're hurt," she said.

"I'm fine."

"You're not fine. Your head has been split
open."

"It will heal."

"You probably have a concussion."

"I'm fine. I'm thinking clearly. I was able
to drive us here."

Admittedly, his vision was growing blurry.

"It's just… It's just the media. We didn't
have to run from them."

Her words scraped him raw. "I am protect-
ing you. And myself."

"They're going to print whatever they want
anyway. Whether they have a picture of you
or not."

But he couldn't bear their questions. He
couldn't. He didn't know why he felt that with
such certainty, only that he did.

"Here," he said, the edges of his vision
darker now. "There's the house."

"Do you have staff here?"

He shook his head. "No. There will be no
one here. We can… Bring people out. Get
food."

His speech was beginning to slur, his mind beginning to turn slower. He couldn't remember quite why they had been running. Only that he had felt like a hunted animal. Only that it had reminded him so starkly of the unending, unforgiving grief that he had experienced when Seraphina had died that he felt overrun with it.

Because that had been the darkest day of his life. Because it had been when he had discovered that his father was wrong about everything. Everything.

He suddenly felt gripped with nausea.

He got out of the car, and wiped blood away from his face. He looked down at his hands, the edges of his vision growing ever darker. And then he vomited onto the grass.

"Matias," she said, moving over to him, throwing her arms around his back. "You have a head injury."

"I just hit my head, that's all. Let's go inside."

"I have to get back to London. I can't be out here. In the middle of nowhere. And you need to go to a hospital."

"I am not going anywhere. Not as long as that pack of hyenas is after us."

"I agree, it's terrible. But surely we can get

another vehicle. We can go back to my apartment. We can—"

"We will stay here."

He went to the front door, and entered his code, the doors giving for him as he ushered her inside.

"What is this?"

"One of my places. A place where I can go for privacy. I don't like everyone to know everything about me. I like them to think that they do."

"Oh. Of course."

It was austere inside. Like him. It was the truth of him, unlike the apartment she had stayed in last night.

"We have got to stop the bleeding on your face. Sit down."

He obeyed her, mostly because he was dizzy. This was an infuriating time to discover his own mortality.

"I'm sitting," he said.

"Yes, you are. Do you have a doctor?"

"What kind of question is that?"

"I assume that rich men like you have doctors who will drop everything and come see to them, is that correct?"

He waved a hand. "Of course it is."

"Then we need to call your doctor. And get

him out here immediately, because I might be able to stop the bleeding but I'm not going to be able to stitch you back together."

"Soon," he said.

He heard her retreat. And when she returned, she had a large white towel. She pressed it over his eyes, his forehead, and he leaned back against the chair, trying to relax.

She held it there, counting, whispering.

"It'll be all right," she said.

He remembered, with a start, what she had said about caring for her mother. He could definitely feel that energy now. That familiarity that she had with the medical.

He didn't know how he felt about it. If he needed medical care, then there was a professional to do it. This wasn't her job. And she had been hurt...

"You're sure you're all right?" he asked.

"Yes," she said softly. "I'm fine."

"I feel like we don't know that for sure."

"I know it well enough," she said. And when she removed the towel from his forehead, and when he opened his eyes he found that he could see nothing at all.

CHAPTER NINE

AUGGIE WAS COMPLETELY SHAKEN. Everything that happened this morning felt jarring and shocking. From them fleeing London, to ending up at this manor house. In the accident...

She had hit her head, but not as badly as he had. The impact had ended up on his side, because he had cranked the wheel sharply and taken her out of harm's way. The gash on his forehead was severe, but she was more worried about the trauma that the impact might've caused.

And now he was looking at her, his dark eyes fixed at a spot just beyond her.

"What?"

"I can't see," he said.

"What do you mean you can't see?" She was so aware that she was stupidly repeating his words like a Muppet, and she couldn't stop herself.

"Just what I said," he ground out. "I cannot see anything."

"We need to call your doctor."

Panic shot through her. This had to be very bad. And it was entirely possible that there was an injury to his brain.

"You can get into my phone. The doctor's name is Carlos Valdes."

She grabbed hold of his phone, which had his blood on it. She grimaced. Then she turned it toward his face and unlocked it, the way that she had done before with his girlfriends. Had that been only a week ago? Had that been the same life even? He didn't seem like the same man. She didn't feel like the same woman. She hadn't even had a moment to try and fully comprehend what had passed between them last night, and now she had to… She just had to save his life.

She called the doctor. "Hello. I am with Matias Balcazar. We are at his country estate in England. I assume you have the address on file." The receptionist on the other end of the phone confirmed. "He's been in an accident, and we need a trauma team to come out right away. Fly if you can. He cannot go to a hospital. He needs to be treated here if you can." He was a billionaire. She knew that he could be treated here. They would bring equipment. "He has a head injury. He cannot see. Please."

"A team including Dr. Valdes is being dispatched immediately," the woman said. "Not to worry."

"How long will they be?"

"Fifteen minutes. They will go by helicopter."

"Thank you," she said.

She hung up, looking around the room, trying to avoid looking at him. Because it made her stomach cramp painfully. Then she sat down, looking straight ahead, in the chair next to his. "I'm right here," she said.

At least the bleeding had stopped on his forehead gash. Though the wound was angry and deep. "They'll be here soon."

"I'm being punished," he said.

"For what?"

"Because I'm not any different than him. And perhaps God is making things right. I blamed my father. I set out to destroy him. Perhaps true justice is understanding that if I am to destroy him for what was done, then I have to destroy myself."

"Stop. Don't get nihilistic. You just have to live through this."

"If I can't see, I don't know that I want to live."

"Stop it. Many people live without their sight. Or various other senses. Do you think that they shouldn't live?"

"I didn't say that."

"You didn't. Because you don't mean that. Which means on some level you must understand that whatever happens, you will learn to live. You will."

"Perhaps I'm tired. Tired of learning to live in new realities."

"Don't get self-pitying. It's only going to make it worse."

"You have a bruise on your cheek. Don't speak to me about self-pity."

"Matias. You didn't deserve for this to happen to you. And you will… You will be all right."

"You don't know that."

She didn't. She was actually just afraid that he was going to suddenly die on her. If something was wrong enough in his brain to take his sight away, who knew what else could suddenly happen. He could have a stroke. Or something. Old anxiety churned through her, along with new.

That she had watched her mother die in

spite of all the advancements in modern medicine, grabbed hold of her now. As she looked at the one man she had ever been intimate with, and watched as he seemed mortal for the first time since she had ever met him. Then she heard the sound of rotor blades outside.

"Thank God."

The next piece of time was a flurry of activity. A stretcher was brought in, and Matias was moved upstairs. There was equipment that came in behind them. And a medical team assembled.

She wanted to follow them, but they kept her sitting downstairs, as they began to examine her.

"You were also in the accident?" the nurse asked, touching Auggie's cheek. "It looks like you were injured."

"Yes. But I'm fine."

She was checked over nonetheless. And given a clean bill of health. Nothing but the contusion on her face.

At that point, Dr. Valdes came back down the stairs.

"Augusta Fremont. You are the one who called for me?"

"Yes. I'm… I'm his fiancée."

She was. For all intents and purposes. And she was going to use that here.

"We will keep a team here overnight. The concern of course is that the swelling will get worse, and we will have to fly him back to the city to do brain surgery."

"He doesn't want to go back. He was... He was bound and determined to leave the city."

It occurred to her that he probably didn't want brain surgery either. And she was arguing about medical emergencies that nobody in the room had any control over.

"We will do our best to treat him here. A scan shows that he has swelling in the brain, centered on the optic nerves. Once pressure is relieved, it is highly likely his sight will return."

"Do you see this often?"

"No. But... It is not unheard of. The concern would be that there's a possibility for a bleed, or a stroke."

"Oh."

"He is very alert. But... His vision."

"And what if it doesn't return?"

"That I would assume that the damage done through the compression of the optic nerve isn't readily repairable. But we would do surgery to see."

"I see."

"If he makes it through the night, then he is undoubtedly stable."

"If he makes it through the night?"

"Without coding. I will not let him die. Don't worry. We'll just see if he needs assistance to continue to live."

"It's not fair," she said. "He hasn't done anything. He didn't...he didn't cause this— the paparazzi were after him. It isn't fair."

"Unfortunately, in my line of work, what I have learned is that often the good die and the bad live. Pickled by bitterness and deceit. I do my best to try and even the playing field."

She didn't know quite what to do, she wanted to go to him, but there was a team up there. She was his fiancée, publicly, and yet she wasn't. But she was his lover. She was his lover and... That night didn't even feel real. Because the fantasy had been shattered in such a cruel way.

Finally, when she was entirely alone downstairs, she called the work wives.

They were still in the office, and each picked up at their desks. "Auggie?" Lynna asked. "Where have you been?"

"In an accident."

Everyone made loud exclamations, and began asking questions all at once.

"I'm with Matias. He's been injured."

"You see the headlines. It's awful. Stories about his sister's overdose, and apparently there's a recording of his final conversation with her. And he told her that if she continued on being an addict that everyone would be better off without her."

Auggie's heart clenched. "He feels... He feels responsible," she said. "And now I know why. But I know that there were other circumstances leading up to her death."

"His father is playing the victim, painting him as a Machiavellian madman who always planned to put a rift in the family, who was part of his own sister's destruction, and who then actively worked against his father. Basically, they're saying that everything he has pretended to be all this time is a lie."

"Well, it is," Auggie said. "He's hurt."

"Oh, no," Maude said.

She noticed the other two didn't react. "He isn't everything they're saying," Auggie said. "I know he's not. You just have to trust me. His father is a terrible man. And no, Matias isn't everything that he appears to be. And he does feel like he has some responsibility to take for his sister's death. But it isn't like that. His father is the one who manipulated his children. He treated his daughter like trash. And he treated Matias... He made him feel like he didn't have another choice but to do all of his bidding all the time."

"Everybody has a choice," Irinka said.

"But some choices are harder to make depending on where you're from."

Irinka looked at her sharply, but didn't say anything.

"I'll keep you all posted," she said.

They all got off the phone, and she breathed out heavily. Then her phone rang again. Just Irinka.

Not on a video call. Auggie picked it up. "Yes?"

"You slept with him, didn't you?"

"What makes you ask me that?"

"Because you're so sure of him. And because you're clearly staying wherever he is."

And not giving details on his injuries. Because she felt protective. She trusted her friends completely, and yet she found she couldn't talk about what had happened today.

"I didn't see why I shouldn't. Since he was going to be part of my reputation either way."

"This is a disaster for us, Auggie. You realize that, don't you?"

"Not if we stick it out," Auggie said. "Because I don't believe that he's a bad person. And I do believe that it will all come together in the end. I do."

"Why do you believe that?"

"Because I have to. Because…" Because she had already watched her mother die. Because she had built this up from nothing, and she wasn't foolish enough, or naïve enough, or even traditional enough to buy into the idea that she could have a happy ending here with him just because the idea was nice. But she did believe that she was a better judge of character than all that. She did believe that the man that she had gone to bed with was a decent one. She believed that he was the good guy, and she just wanted to believe that things were going to be okay. But she knew from experience that they might not be.

That his father was the bad guy. And she wanted to be part of making sure the world knew it too. She didn't know how to explain all of that to Irinka.

"It isn't just that I'm attracted to him," she said softly.

"I hope not."

"He's hurt, I can't leave him now. And if I do, it will be even worse for us."

"Undoubtedly."

"Trust me. Trust me please. That I can fix this."

"I will. Because you're my friend. Because you haven't been wrong about moves with the business before. But it does kind of seem like every wrong thing has included him."

"I know. So just let me… Let me see it through."

"Where will it end? Are you going to marry him? Have his babies?"

The idea made her feel warm.

"No. But let me help him rebuild."

"Okay, Auggie."

She hung up the phone, and stood there, staring out the window at the back garden for a very long time. She didn't want to believe that she had ruined everything with this. But it was possible that she had.

But for now, she was going to do what she could for Matias. Because the truth was, she had thrown her lot in with him, and she had to see it through.

And more than that… She cared about him. Because she knew what it was like to be alone in the world. And she had her friends. He had his money. It wasn't enough. She knew that it wasn't.

She took a deep breath and her chest ached.

Then she sat down in that same chair she had been in beside him earlier. And she drifted off to sleep.

CHAPTER TEN

WHEN HE WOKE up the medical staff was ready to leave.

"It's been forty-eight hours of observation," the doctor said. "You are well, but there is still an issue with the optic nerve."

"That's why I can't see?"

"Yes. I would rather not rush into brain surgery. Because the recovery can be punishing. I would rather see if it will resolve on its own."

"How long will you give it?"

"A couple of weeks at least. At that point, we will take you in for further testing."

"And in the meantime?"

"You are a billionaire. I assume you have the resources."

He knew the doctor was being practical, and not dismissive, but Matias still found himself in rage.

"I am in the middle of a crisis of image."

"You have bigger issues. You will have to physically recover."

There were flashes of light in his vision at times, but he wasn't entirely sure if he was hallucinating them or not. There was the occasional blurred edge. And again, he wasn't certain if that was real or not. "Stay here," the doctor said. "Your fiancée will take care of you."

His fiancée…

"Auggie is here?"

"Yes. She has been pacing the halls and barely sleeping. She clearly cares about you a great deal."

Well. Auggie had managed to convince the doctor that her feelings for him were real. If only he knew the truth. Auggie was here because it benefited her. Because the truth was, she couldn't abandon him now. It was too late. Her reputation was already twined together with his. It was a self-sustaining problem at this point.

"You know I can be here in under twenty minutes if you have need."

And with that, he was left to his own devices. Without the constant beeping of monitors. And without his vision.

He heard footsteps, though he could not

figure out where they were coming from. He didn't know this place well enough. That was the problem. If they were in his apartment in London, he would have a better sense of the direction of everything. Of course, if he was in London he would have to listen for the sounds of the city, and out here it was distressingly quiet.

"I overheard."

Auggie. He thought of her sitting in the passenger seat, that bruise on her cheek. But then again, in his arms, naked. Beautiful. He held onto that image. He held onto it tightly.

"Then you know he thinks that I'll be fine."

"That isn't quite what he said. But, yes."

"You will have to take care of me," he said. What a lowering realization.

"I will," she said.

"I need you to tell me what the press is writing about me."

"I don't see how that's going to help you."

"Because I want to know."

He was suddenly consumed with helplessness. He knew that there were many ways that people without sight navigated the world, but he didn't know any of them. He knew that there were ways to use technology when you are visually impaired, but he had not learned how to do that. He had no skills for navigating this, and he had no idea what he was supposed to do.

He suddenly felt replete with rage and helplessness. If she chose not to show him, he wouldn't be able to find it for himself.

"I need to be able to trust you," he said.

"Can you trust me to tell you that you maybe don't want to know?"

"No," he said.

"Okay," she said, cautious. "Well, you're just going to have to deal with it."

"Do not play with me," he said.

"I'm not playing with you," she responded. She sounded exasperated. He couldn't know for sure. He couldn't see her.

"I will not heal," he said.

"You just thought that it wasn't an option for you to remain like this."

"But I will. Because this is what it was like for my sister. I'm certain. She slipped into darkness. Alone. And here I am, doomed to a life of darkness, and I will not even be granted the release of death to soften this."

"Is that what you think? You think that death would be a release?"

"From this? What is the point of any of it. Perhaps this is what I have been avoiding all this time. To defeat my father is to defeat myself. Everything that I have done, everything is to try and avenge the death of my sister. But the truth is, in order to fully avenge her, I must take myself down as well. And now the world has done it for me."

"Stop it," she said. He could not see what she did, but he heard a clattering. "You are… You are offensive. Do you think that you're being punished? You think that this accident was some sort of light brought upon you. You didn't die when your brain swelled up, maybe you could be grateful for that."

"I find it difficult to be grateful," he said.

"Clearly," she said. "Clearly you find it difficult to be grateful. But I find myself sorely lacking in sympathy for you. Let me ask you this question. Do you think that my mother deserved cancer?"

He frowned. "No. What does your mother have to do with this?"

"Your logic indicates that you think that people are struck down because they deserve it. You were spared. Perhaps you can focus on the fact that you didn't die. Maybe you can figure out all the ways in which you deserve to live."

"You don't understand," he said. "I have

dedicated my life to avenging my sister's death."

"So you've said." He heard her voice soften slightly. She sat down. At least, he was fairly certain he recognized the sound of her sitting. "Tell me. From the beginning. Tell me how all of this was supposed to avenge her."

He stared at nothing. He had no other choice. He was enveloped in darkness. He felt the wall that he had built up inside of himself erode, crumble. And all of the acrid, toxic emotions that he had been holding at bay for all these years poured out. Poured forth.

"I needed to do everything in my power to be different from him. Not simply to make myself a better person, I'm beyond redemption, and I am aware of that. I decided to prove to him that everything he had done was pointless. That allowing his daughter to die, alienating his son, and turning his wife into a ghost of a human being, all of those things were unnecessary to his success. I set out to do that by being the antithesis of everything that he was."

"And that's why your reputation for treating women well, for being good, that's why that reputation matters. Not because you have an investment in being good."

"I am not good. Have you not paid attention to anything that I've said? I am beyond help."

"All right. What else then? What else have you done to try and avenge your sister."

"All of this. Everything that I am. I intended to destroy his empire. Eclipse it with my own. I intended to… To be something he never could be. Which was loved by the public. Not because I… Not because I deserved it, not because I even wanted it. Because he said it couldn't be done, and what better way to win, than by beating him while not playing his game at all?"

"Right. So, with this headline, you understand that everything you are is called into question."

"I am aware," he snarled.

"I'm not sure that it's fixable."

She might as well have dropped a boulder on his chest. He felt as if it had caved in. "And what is the point of anything?"

"You're going to have to figure that out. I can't tell you what the point of your life is. But you're going to have to ask yourself a very serious question. What if you can't win?"

"That isn't an option," he said, rejecting it instantly.

"I'm sorry, you can sit here and tell me that

you deserve to be blinded for the rest of your life, deserve this accident, but you cannot take on board the fact that you might fail at your mission."

"No," he said. "It is my purpose."

"It's not your purpose. It is somebody else's purpose. You don't have a purpose. The only thing that you do is react. To the death of your sister, to the bastard behavior of your father. That's it. To the headlines the paparazzi print about you, to all of these things. You shape your life around them."

"You know nothing," he said, wanting to turn and face her, not entirely certain where she was. "You know nothing. You are a child. You lost someone, and for that I am sorry. But it is nothing compared to what I went through."

"Oh, are we doing that? Are we measuring trauma? The reason my trauma seems smaller than yours is because I've done something to deal with it rather than sitting in self-pity for the past several years."

"Self-pity. Is that what you think this is? It is not self-pity that I have remade myself into an instrument of my father's destruction. It is not self-pity. It is the only way that I can find a shred of sense in the fact that I draw breath still. And now… I know there is no sense to it whatsoever."

He bent down and picked up something, he didn't know what, and threw it as hard as he could. He heard the sound of cracking glass, and Auggie gasped.

"You are a child," she shouted. "Sit in here by yourself then. I'll come bring you food when I think you're hungry."

More of her making decisions for him.

"You cannot leave me," he raged.

"I can and I will. Because you are a self-pitying fool. I put myself on the line trying to help you. And you might be unfixable, Matias Balcazar. Not because you're blind, but because you can't see a life that extends beyond playing this game with your father. This is where it got you. You are here because of you. Not because of fate, not because of God, not even because of your dad. You are here because you couldn't handle sitting in your own discomfort without doing something. You had to react. And that's what you've been doing all along."

"You don't know me. You can't tell me what I've been doing for all these years when you weren't even around until a couple of months ago."

"I could leave you up here," she said. "I could leave you up here to rot. And frankly, at this point, I wouldn't even be sorry."

Then he heard something clattered to the ground. Her ring, he realized. It was followed by angry footsteps and a slamming door. She had genuinely left him there.

He growled, to the empty space. And he wished she was there for him to growl at.

The anger came from somewhere deep inside of him, and he had not given voice to such darkness in more years than he could count. But he was the darkness now. Surrounded by it. It was outside of him, and within. It was... It was untenable.

He stood motionless, uncertain of which way to go. And then he began to slowly walk with his hands outstretched, trying to get a gauge for everything in the room. He ran into a side table, and he cursed. He felt for furniture, the smooth surface, down the sides. Then he moved and found the bed, his hands moving over the blankets. He decided that was good enough for now. He sat down on the edge of the mattress. He wanted alcohol, but he would need her to get it for him. He didn't have his phone, and even if he did, he didn't know how to use it in his present state.

It really did remind him of the day that Seraphina had died. Because even then he had felt helpless. Useless. Frozen.

And responsible all at the same time.

If he had said something different to her. If he had not said anything to her at all.

He had broken the one person that loved him.

The one person he had loved.

And now there was nothing. Nothing at all. Nothing but this void. But this black hole of need. He had tried to cover it all up. He had managed to find a façade that had... Let him live.

He might not have ever truly taken the joy in life that he pretended to, but it had been better than this.

There had been noise. Distraction. And it might not have ever penetrated down to his soul, but it kept him moving.

The stillness... He despised it.

And right now, he despised Augusta Fremont. A convenient target for his rage. For refusing to do his bidding.

The personification of how the world had turned against him, rather than bending to his will.

He sat there in the darkness, and he understood. Profoundly, the urge to take a substance that might remove you from your reality. Remove you from everything.

If it had been in his hands, he might've done so.

It was a rock bottom he had never faced down before. Because he had always had something to do. He'd always had a mission.

And now that mission was gone.

CHAPTER ELEVEN

SHE WAS BEGINNING to feel guilty. It wasn't fair to be so mean to him. Maybe. But he was… Maybe she needed to feel sorry for him. Maybe. She had known that the playboy thing was a façade, but it was a horrible thing to lift the lid on and find nothing more than despair underneath it. Darkness. That was what he was. He was a black hole. And she had just left him up there.

She was beginning to calm down now. The truth was, she didn't care about what this did to the business's reputation. It would actually be pretty easy to get out of it. What had been revealed about him was a big family secret, and since nobody had known about him, she would have plausible deniability also.

She sighed, and she put in a group call to the work wives.

"I have to stay here," she said.

"Of course you do," Irinka said.

"You seem alarmingly okay with it."

"Is he still... Is he still blind?" Irinka asked.

"Yes."

"And it's completely understandable that you can't leave."

She pinched the bridge of her nose. "The thing is, I either need to completely cut bait with him, and say that I was taken in, I didn't realize that he had such a dark past, or... Or I'm all in."

"What do you think about him?" Lynna asked.

"I think that the situation is a lot more complicated than the media is making it out to be. I think that he's a mess. He's certainly not the world's favorite boyfriend. And he's not a golden retriever. But we already knew that." She paused. "I don't think I realized how much of it was a conscious façade."

"You have our support," Maude said. "Of course you can't abandon him in his hour of need. He's a real person, and so are you. You aren't just a business, or reputation."

"Well, I'm not very happy to end up caregiving for somebody again. I didn't ask for this."

"Of course you didn't," Lynna said. "But since when does the world care if you asked for something or not?"

"I keep thinking that maybe I'd earned an easy stretch, Lynna."

Lynna laughed. "Oh, Auggie. None of us can earn that."

"Well then what's the point?" Auggie asked, feeling flat and exceptionally angry at whoever had made the rules of life, because they really weren't working for her right now.

Why was she attached to him?

Maude was right, it wasn't just about business.

And she felt slightly feral with that realization. Because she hadn't asked for this. Any more than she had asked to love a mother who was slowly dying for years. Any more than she had asked to be the one who had to bear the burden of that love, of that care.

She curled her hands into fists and tried to calm herself down. She didn't like this part of herself. The one that would get so awash in her own tragedy. She wasn't the one who had been sick, just like she wasn't the one who was experiencing temporary blindness now.

But it hurt her. And there was no place for it to go, and maybe that was the problem.

She had not asked to care about this man. He was a registered disaster. She knew bet-

MILLIE ADAMS   165

ter than to like him, even the slightest bit, and yet she did.

Worse, she had gone and made him her first lover.

"I need to go," she said, shaking her head.

"Are you okay?"

"No," she said. "I am very deeply not okay. This has been the weirdest week of my life. And… I am enmeshed. In a way that I really wish I wasn't, but I am. And… I'm woman enough to take responsibility for it. But that doesn't mean I don't feel horrendously sorry for myself."

"I like a little bit of self-pity, personally," Irinka said. "Take care of yourself. And you know if you need anything we'll be right there for you."

"Just hold down the fort. I don't know what kind of storm is awaiting you all in terms of media."

"We'll handle it. Our official stance, of course, is that we support you, and your judgment. So anything to do with him is likely a gross exaggeration. Also, if you want me to dig up dirt on his father…"

"You don't need to go that far," said Auggie. "However, if dirt presents itself…"

"Mudslinging typically just gets everyone dirty," Maude said.

"But it's sometimes necessary," Lynna said. "Because life is unpredictable that way."

"Indeed." She said goodbye to her friends, and then returned to staring out the window. She closed her eyes, imagining the press of his mouth against hers. Imagining the way that he had touched her just a couple of nights ago. How she had felt him moving inside of her.

How had they gone from that to this?

It was supposed to be a fantasy. She had accepted that it would be a temporary fantasy, but she really hadn't had any clue that it would be… That it would be so temporary. They were supposed to have their two months to act as an engaged couple. They were supposed to…

There was no supposed to. She just had to get over it. That was life.

Her father had been a genetic material donor and nothing more. Her mother was dead. There was nobody left in the world that really loved her. She had her friends, and she was grateful for that, but there was no real… Family. And it wasn't supposed to be that way, but it was. She had given her virginity to the first gorgeous man that she had found herself in proximity with who wanted her, and now he was injured. It wasn't supposed to be that way. But it was.

She knew better than to be fanciful, she knew better than to be a whiny brat about it.

But it was going to start with him not being a whiny brat.

She closed her eyes and willed herself to move. She made some sandwiches and packed them away into a basket. She looked outside at the sun. It was a beautiful day. A beautiful day in England, for God's sake.

They were going to take advantage of it. She was going to keep him from sinking into despair, partly because she needed to keep herself from doing it. She didn't have the time to be self-pitying. So she wouldn't allow him to be either.

She stamped up the stairs, and flung the door open to his room. He was sitting on the end of the bed, and the expression of desolation on his face caught hard in her throat.

"You aren't doing this," she said.

"Excuse me?"

"You aren't sinking into the abyss, Matias. Not while I'm here."

He had the audacity to lounge back on the

bed, looking in her direction like he was a particularly uninterested cat. And she knew that he couldn't see her, and yet, his dark gaze felt penetrating.

She was a bit annoyed for thinking the word *penetrating*.

She gritted her teeth. "Did you have commentary?" she asked.

"I have nothing to say. But I do not know what you think is happening here. Are you a schoolmarm? Do you seek to whip me in shape? Or perhaps you haven't realized that it's too late for that. I am beyond redemption."

"Well, unhappily for you, I don't believe in that. I don't believe that people are garbage. I don't believe that people are to be disposed of just because they have made some mistakes."

"Mistakes. You say that as if I have gotten a poor grade on a math test, not said the very wrong thing that sent my sister to her grave."

"You didn't inject her with the drugs."

His face turned sharply, as if she had slapped him.

"I'm sorry, but it's true. You're taking away her agency in all of this. Yes, your father was horrible, and he clearly made her feel bad about herself, but he obviously manipulated you too. He is still doing it. You're doing it back, but so is he. You're engaged in this ridiculous, un-winnable game with a man who just sounds... Frankly awful. Even now, he's exploiting his daughter's death to hurt you. To hurt your perception in the public eye, I don't even think it's about your feelings. He probably isn't even aware that you have them. He probably doesn't consider feelings at all. That is a horrible thing. An utterly horrifying proposition."

The growing realization inside of her felt so big that she couldn't stop. She was trying to read his face to see if this surprised him as much as it did her. She was... Undone.

"So what if you let him win. What if you let him have this. Because what is there to say? Do you continue to rake over the ground of your sister's death so that the public can be satisfied that what happened was just a horrible mistake. Anybody reading the article is going to understand that. Is going to understand that she was a woman who was troubled because of... Because of her upbringing. But if she was troubled because of her upbringing then so were you."

"No," he said. "That isn't true. I... I should've been stronger."

"Why? Why should you have been stronger, Matias? It doesn't make any sense."

"Because I was stronger. Inherently."

"Why? Because the way that you lived, and the things that you did were closer to what your father found acceptable? It seems to me like you were a child who could simply do the things laid out before him, and because of that you avoided the worst of what your father was, until you fully realized just how monstrous of a man he was. Your sister couldn't fall in line, so she didn't have those years of being able to fool herself. But what you did was not easier, and it doesn't mean that he was any kinder to you. It just didn't manifest itself in the same way."

"I am stronger, and I should've been stronger for her. I should've realized. I should have had insight."

"You didn't. You were just a child. Even if you were twenty years old, you were a child. Under your father's thumb, with no real sense of the world and how it was. So I'm going to ask you again. What if you let him win? Because what do you gain by continuing to fight this? At least right now. At least now... You're free. Because here we are, out in the middle of nowhere, and we aren't going to let anyone know what's happening."

"It will look as if I'm hiding."

"That's fine. I've asked the work wives to handle it. They will. The thing is, your grief has just been dredged up to the surface, and it's actually completely all right if you don't engage in playing games with the media to get back at your father."

He was silent for a moment. "They will think that my silence is an admission of guilt."

"Some people will. But when we actually do speak, perhaps people will see this for what it is. You're the one that actually cares. You're the one that can't bear to use your sister's memory like this."

"Everything I do is for my sister's memory."

"I know that. But that's different. It's different than this. Different than the way that he is trying to destroy you over the top of her story. Her reputation."

"Perhaps you're right."

"I have made us a picnic. And I think that we should have it."

His expression contorted into one of horror. "I do not want to go on a picnic. I don't want to go on a picnic even when I can see, much less so now. Are you going to lead me around like a stumbling fool in the daisies? With a basket?"

"There are no daisies."

His lip curled in disgust. "What is the purpose of this?"

"I think that the purpose of it, perhaps, is to get you out of your own head. You are not going to heal as long as you're sitting here in distress."

"I am not in distress."

"You could've fooled me. You were, only moments ago threatening to drink yourself to death. I think maybe some perspective is in order."

"I think you might need to be able to see in order to have perspective."

"And I think that you are being a cantankerous fool."

"Enough," he said sharply. "I will have a picnic with you. But you must endeavor to be less ridiculous."

"Oh, well I'll try."

She walked over to the bed and rested her hand against his. Instantly, the contact between them sent an arrow of desire through her. She wanted him. Still. In the stillness, the silence, the space of this moment, she might even want him more than she had that night when it was a fantasy. Pure and perfect and lovely.

This was sharp, awful and weighted.

And yet…

She felt lonely, standing there touching his hand, looking at him, wishing that they could be closer, wishing that she could be further away. She saw something like desolation in his dark eyes and she wondered if he felt it too.

"Come on," she said, tugging his hand gently.

He stood, and she laced her fingers through his. "I'll make sure that you get there okay."

"And I have to trust that you're not leading me into a field of daisies."

"Most people would be more worried about a hornet's nest."

"Not me. I'm much more concerned about softness."

"Well, that is an interesting thing to hear you say. Especially considering your apartment is one of the softest places I've ever been."

"You know that's for the women who come to visit."

"Maybe the daisies are for me," she said. She did her best not to dwell on the reality of other women visiting him. She had seen those other women. She had seen them in bed together. Of course, it felt different now. Sharp.

She held on to him more firmly, and began to lead him out of the room. "Two more steps and then we're at the stairs," she said.

"Thank you."

There was a hardness to his tone, and she could tell that he wasn't happy that he had to be led.

"It is temporary," she said. "You'll be just fine."

"You don't know that."

"No. I don't. But I used to say it to my mother all the same. I told her that she would be fine, and then I told her that I would be fine. Because what else are you supposed to say? That I don't know?" Her heart started to beat faster. He kept in step with her, as if the familiarity that he had with stairs helped. But of course he had one hand on her, one on the railing, and she did her level best to keep him steady. He must hate this. But she hated it too. Hated being put in this position again. Hated that he wouldn't even let her give him the lip service that would at least make her feel better.

"What are you supposed to say to someone? That you might not be fine? That it might be like this for you forever. It might be. Maybe you won't be okay. None of us will be." She let out a heavy sigh, and her foot reached the bottom of the stairs. "It's just floor now. You stand here, I'm going to go into the kitchen and get food."

"What if I don't wish to wait?"

"That's too bad. There are going to be concessions that you have to make. That I have to make."

She went and she picked up the basket of food, and stood there for a moment. She took a deep breath. And she tried to make some sense out of her feelings. Her utterly selfish, uncharitable, mixed-up feelings. Because she wanted to kiss him, and she wanted to shake him, and she wanted to go and find a doctor and rail at them for not fixing him immediately, because she also hated seeing him helpless. As much as she hated seeing him hopeless.

She took a deep breath, and went back out to where he was. "I'm here," she said.

He didn't reach his hand out for her, she went and grabbed it. "Come on," she said, propelling him toward the door.

"You have too much power over me," he said.

She paused for a moment. "Well, that's unusual."

"I am aware that I generally enjoy an out-sized amount of power. I do not enjoy the loss of it."

"You never really had it," she said, tugging him out the door. "I mean, if it makes you feel better. That's one thing you learn when you have a parent who gets ill. Or, if you ever get hurt. Or sick. We live under the illusion of having control. That if we do certain things our lives will turn out a certain way. But it isn't true. Even I have fallen back into that belief system. I guess it's just been too long since life coldcocked me. Not so much right now."

"Does my injury inconvenience you?"

"I already said that it did," she said. "I'm not trying to be mean. I'm not. It's only... Whatever power you thought you had, it was never real."

He let out a hard, short laugh. "I suppose not."

"It doesn't mean that your father is in control over you. Also, you're a billionaire, so technically, you don't even need the public to like you. You could just step away from everything, never work again."

"But don't you understand how that feels... Wrong."

The sun was shining through the trees, and it really was a beautiful day outside. There were no daisies, but there were other wild-flowers, and she was tempted to drag him through them. No one would ever know, least of all him. She didn't, though. Instead, she walked with him to the shade of a large, ex-pansive willow. She spread a blanket out on the ground, and then guided him down to sit beside her. It was beautiful. But, much like everything in her life, it was the simile of something tranquil. Because this wasn't the truth of it. He was here under sufferance, they were hiding from a rabid media. She was his keeper more than anything else, and the fact that she had been his lover probably meant nothing to him.

It meant everything to her.

It had been a singular experience as far as she was concerned.

And of course for him… It had basically just been a Tuesday.

He might've even forgotten that they'd slept together. He had hit his head, after all, and it might have been any woman.

Really, it might have been any woman.

"It is not because of work ethic," he said. "Not because of a need to succeed. It is simply that my sister is no longer alive. And if I don't do something, if I don't make something of myself, of my life, or destroy what remains of my father, what was the purpose of anything?"

"I don't know." She felt immeasurably sad, a sense of dread hollowing out her chest. "I don't know. It's something I certainly haven't figured out. All I know to do is to keep going."

She looked down at the kingdom blanket, at her hand, so close to his. But not touching. Not now that they didn't have to.

"Maybe we don't have to solve any of life's mysteries right now. Maybe you just need to heal."

He snorted. "I have never sat idle."

"You don't really have a choice. Your body is sort of commanding that you do it. So maybe you need to listen. Maybe you need to heed the lesson."

"Maybe you are too."

She snapped her head around to look at him. "I'm sorry what?"

"Maybe you are meant to rest."

"I'm taking care of you."

"I suppose it is in your best interest to make sure I don't fall and hit my head. Again."

"Who knows, maybe another knock on the head would cure you."

"I very much doubt it."

She stared at the side of his face. "Are you really suggesting that I take a rest?"

"Well, you asked me, what is my life if I'm not trying to defeat my father? I don't know the answer to that question. But what is your life. If not putting a great distance between yourself and who you once were?"

Auggie didn't know what to say to that. "I'm not doing that consciously."

But here, sitting in the space that was so reminiscent of being a caregiver all those years ago, she felt uncomfortable. More than uncomfortable. She felt trapped, in many ways. She felt afraid. Like she was never actually going to find her way out of this. Like she was regressed. So maybe he was right. Maybe that was her life. Putting as much distance between herself and the scared girl she had been.

Except… No. He was right. It was why she had never slowed down to take a lover, or sightsee when she was doing business travels, or any of the other very normal things that most people her age did, and had done.

She had her friends. She loved them dearly. But she had gathered them up on her way forward, and they had helped propel her. She didn't only love them for what they did for her, but the fact remained, they had been part of her goals. And when was the last time she had done anything that wasn't about... Those goals. Getting somewhere new, somewhere further away. Somewhere exciting. It had been him. The night that she had spent with him had been the one nod to herself as a whole woman, to just feeling good, to just enjoying life.

It had been the only time.

"Well, I guess there were worse things than taking a break here in a beautiful home."

"Is it beautiful?"

"You've been here before. You could see when we arrived."

"Still. Where are we sitting now?"

She began to unpack their sandwiches. "We are sitting beneath a sweeping, green willow tree. The leaves are light green. We are sitting on a blue kingdom blanket. The grass is darker than the willow tree. I steered us around the clutch of white flowers that we might have sat in. But they're there. Off in the distance. Not so close that they'll get their softness all over you. The sky is uncharacteristically blue. The clouds are round and fat and white. It is a glorious day. Perfect."

"I smell the flowers."

"They're sweet," she said.

"I don't think I can remember ever pausing to smell flowers before in my life."

"You know, I don't think I have either." She blinked, her eyes stinging. "Actually, I can remember spending a great deal of time trying to get the scent of too many flowers out of my nose. When my mother went into hospice. And old, well-meaning friends sent bouquets. Mostly, those flowers that you get sent from online florists just don't smell very good. It is the same as this. But it is nice to have some of the glorious outside brought in I suppose. When it's the only way you're ever going to experience it again."

"They sent flowers, but did anybody come and help you?"

The question hit her with the unerring quality of an arrow getting to the heart of its target.

There was a difference. One she had never even pulled apart before.

Roses were lovely, but they did not hold you. They didn't help clean or deal with paperwork. They didn't tell you what to do next. They were not company.

She shook her head. "No. Nobody was close

enough to her to do that. Not anymore. After she had me, I think she sort of receded from her life. I don't know if she was embarrassed because of my father or… I don't know. And I can't ask her now. This is the worst part about losing somebody. You get older, and you gain perspective, and there are so many questions that you wish you would've asked. So many ways that you wish you could have known them. I feel devastated by the fact that I will never truly know her. It's the grief that keeps on giving."

"I can understand that. I will never understand what drove my sister to her addiction. Not really. Not the way that I want to. I will never be able to share my experiences of my father with her. She was the only other person to have him as a father. To understand. And I wish… I wish she was here now. Because I would be different with her. Because I know myself, and my father in a way that might allow me to know her."

"I'm sorry," she said. "I think it's cruel. To be robbed of a relationship like that."

"I took it for myself."

"You didn't."

"I did. It was my words. My actions. I just wish that there was another chance. A chance to atone and have it really mean something, rather than just being… A dark, futile thing, that feels like a necessity. It feels like the only way that I deserve to go on breathing."

"Maybe she would want more for you than that. More for you than breathing. Because the really sad thing is… Your sister can't know you better either. If she were here, you can't simply think about how you would be different. But about how she would be different, too. So maybe the version of her that you knew… Who was perhaps very poorly, maybe she couldn't have wanted more or better. But you don't know the woman that she would've become. If she would've been more patient with herself. If she would have given all of it just a little bit more time."

"I thought that I was here to rest. Not engage with all my old ghosts."

"Well. I guess so. But you and I just have so many."

He shifted, and along with his body's movements, she felt something change in the air. "What are you wearing?"

He was done with ghosts, then.

Immediately, heat flooded her cheeks. "What do you mean? What am I wearing?"

"I'm curious. The last time I saw you, you

were wearing that orange dress. The one I had taken off of you the night before."

"Are you back to playing a role?"

"No, but does that surprise you that I would rather think about you, and the encounter that we shared, rather than the death of my sister?"

"Just tell me. Really. Are you doing this because it makes you comfortable, or are you asking because you… Because you want me?"

"I want you."

She swallowed hard. Her heart was thundering. And she considered. Considered what this meant for her. Considered if this meant that she should indulge him or not. Because they were here alone. For all this time. He couldn't see. But that didn't mean that he couldn't…

"I'm wearing a white dress. And I will say that it is somewhat see-through. It comes up above my knees. And it has a scooped neckline. It is not modest. You can see the… The curves of my breasts." The words came out in a hushed whisper.

"Good," he said.

"You should eat your sandwich."

"What are you wearing underneath it."

She bit the inside of her cheek, and rather than question the wisdom of any of this, she indulged him. She indulged herself.

"A white lace bra. You can see through it. You can see my nipples. And… The panties match. You know… What that probably looks like."

He growled. "I do."

"And now you should eat."

"What if I find it's not food that I'm hungry for."

"Well, you should…"

He found her mouth. Unerringly. Like it was no trouble at all. His lips pressed to hers, and her heart stopped. They were out in the open, but no one else was here. Need was coursing through her body, and she found that she wanted…

She wanted this. She wanted to give him this. There was no one, not for miles. No one would know if they did this out here in the open.

Suddenly, she was gripped by the bitter regret that he wouldn't be able to see this. Them. Beneath a wide, expansive sky.

"I don't need to be able to see to know my way around your body."

She shivered. And at the same time, she felt a pulse of jealousy, because of course she was going to benefit from all the women who had come before her. Of course she was.

"I want you," she whispered. "I want this. Every time you took a woman into that bedroom I wondered. I wondered what you did with her. I wondered how good it felt."

"It felt nothing like being with you," he said. "I have been with more women than I can count. I won't pretend. I won't pretend that I have not... Indulged myself in this way. But it wasn't the same."

"Why?"

"You see me. And right now, in the darkness of my own mind, it is the most... The most bitter thing to say. But you saw something in me that nobody else ever did. And I felt like... When I touched you, was closer to seeing myself. And now, I can see nothing. But there's you. You, and you make me feel like perhaps... I'm not floating and nothing. Like I'm not alone."

"Matias," she whispered, putting her hands on his lips. And then she leaned in and kissed him, consuming him, pushing her tongue deep inside of his mouth like she was a woman who knew full well what she was doing, rather than a woman who was being led by the desire that was clawing at her chest.

"Matias," she whispered.

He wrapped his arms around her waist

and lifted her up, bringing her to straddle his body. Her dress pushed up to the tops of her thighs, and the hard ridge of his arousal pressed firmly against that aching place there. Oh, how she wanted him. Deep inside of her.

She told him so. Whispered against his mouth in the crudest possible way. Felt him surge with pleasure beneath her.

She didn't feel any shame. With him, she never had. With him, it was like she was a new version of herself. Like she was the woman she might have been. If she hadn't always been running. Running and running with no hope of ever stopping. With no reward at the end. No goal but distance. Between herself and the sad girl she'd once been. He was right. But here and now in the bright warmth of the sun, with his hands on her body, she was something else entirely. A new creature, remade beneath the insistence of his touch. It was glorious.

She had felt that urge earlier. To close the distance between them. To really touch him. To not be so alone.

He must feel alone. With everything so dark around him. So she touched him. Everywhere. Moved her hands over his shoulders, down his back. She kissed him, his face, his neck. Until she found herself lying on her back on the blanket with him stripping his clothes off quickly. She moved her hands down that sculpted chest, his ridged stomach. To his proud, glorious masculinity. "You're so beautiful," she said.

"You are too." He moved his hands over her curves. "It doesn't matter that I cannot see. I know it. I feel it. You taste beautiful. The feel of your skin beneath my hands, is beautiful. And I would... I would trade heaven and earth to be able to see. The glory of your skin. The color of your nipples. That beautiful, slick pinkness between your legs. I would give my very soul. But the trouble is I no longer have my soul. But thankfully, I have you."

He said it ragged, his voice rough. She believed every word.

At least, she believed that he did. That he felt soulless. Shrouded in darkness.

So she tried to make her kiss the light. As they came together, as he moved inside of her with quick, decisive strokes that carried her right to heaven, she tried to give him all that sunlight. To pour it into her touch, her kiss.

In every fractured word of pleasure.

She tried.

"Matias," she whispered. "Matias please."

He put his hand between her legs and slid his thumb over her most sensitive place. And she shattered. Screaming out his name all the way up to the sun, the sky, the clouds.

And when she came back down to earth, he was there with her, his forehead pressed to hers as he spilled himself inside of her.

"Dammit," he said, his voice rough. "I forgot to use a condom."

"It's okay," she said. "I'm on the pill. Just as a precaution. I know it's not… Safe, necessarily. But…"

"I would never hurt you," he said.

"I know."

But right then, she knew that wasn't true. He would hurt her. Because in the end they would go their separate ways, and it would tear her into pieces.

But he wouldn't do it on purpose. He just would. Because of who they were.

This wasn't real. And neither were they. How could they be? She was taken out of her life, and he was removed from his. He had even lost some of his senses. Maybe that was part of why they were out here, naked in a field. They had lost their senses.

"Why haven't you been with anyone?" he asked.

"Well, I have now."

"Before. Us... This. It got swallowed up by the accident. By everything."

She lifted a shoulder, but then realized he couldn't see the gesture. "I would've thought that us sleeping together was just a mundane thing to you."

"It wasn't. It meant something. I know you, Auggie, and I can't say the same for any of the other women that I have ever taken as lovers. I respected them, I even liked them in a casual sense, but I didn't know even half about them that I know about you. And I find myself curious."

"I just didn't have the time. And mainly... I don't think I wanted to let anyone in. I had great practice at being a fortress, and it's difficult to be something else. In the last seven years my life has changed relentlessly. Every month, every year has felt different to me."

She plucked at a piece of grass. "When my mother's health declined even more than it already had, I had to be as strong as I possibly could be to get through that. To finish high school while I was taking care of her. I had to grieve her while she sat in front of me. I had to keep going, because you can't stop, because when someone is dying it doesn't stop. It changes by the day. And so do you. I wanted it to stop. There would be a moment when it all felt manageable. Where she wasn't in too much pain, and she was still there, and I would wish that everything could just... Stop. For a moment. And then when it was hard, sometimes I would just wish..."

She swallowed hard, the truth, the honesty, cutting her throat on its way out. "That it was over. But there was no one that I could say that to. Nobody that I could share with. I got used to processing all of that inside myself. While I tried to look okay, tried to be brave. Then my mother died, and I had to learn how to grieve while I kept on walking. Because I had the opportunity to go to school, so I had to keep moving. And I did. Farther away from home with every step. Farther away from who I was, but I was the same, really."

She swallowed hard, her throat feeling tight. "Some days I feel like I've never actually sat down and sorted through all of it, but really, what's the point?" She looked at him, beseeching, even though she knew that he couldn't look back. "When you go through something that painful, isn't it better to just keep going?"

"That's the only way that I know," he said. "But I managed to find the time to have sex."

She laughed. "I dunno. I don't know why it was different for me. Maybe it was just not knowing how to connect with another person."

"Again, I managed to have sex without doing that at all."

"Do you really think so?" she asked. "Do you really think you don't know how to connect with another person?"

"I know I don't. I don't even know how to connect with myself." He smiled. He stared on, unseeing at the flowers that she had told him about but that he hadn't witnessed himself. "Sometimes I wonder if I am hollow. If I became the character that I fashioned for myself. If there's nothing left anymore. Of who I really am. I would almost hope so. Because the man that I was... He was also nothing." She watched as he swallowed hard, his Adam's apple bobbing up and down, a muscle in his jaw jumping. "I was my father's creation then. But what you said earlier haunts me. I am little more than his creation now. Because everything I do is in response to him."

"I didn't say that to be mean," she said. Though she was conscious of the fact that it had been quite mean, and she had been frustrated. "I think it's true of all of us, isn't it?

Our bodies are temples that house our greatest successes and failures, that build altars to our trauma and our tribulations. It's what keeps us going. I think we're all objects forged in the fires of the good and bad things we've been through. We are all just doing things in response to what happened before."

"Let's say I think you're right," he said. "I think I have not lived for myself. And now that I can see nothing… I see that."

"Oh, I'm right now, am I?"

"Yes, and I am sorry I threw the glass. I was not thinking. I could have hurt you and I didn't—"

"You didn't hurt me," she said. "But you can say I'm right again."

"Don't push me."

"Why not? You wouldn't see me coming."

He looked annoyed, and she loved it. She liked sitting with him, talking to him. Teasing him even when they were talking about deadly serious things.

"How do you stop? How do you…get ahead of the action? I think that's what I've been trying to do, and yet, then my father came in and showed that he still has the ability to pull the pin on the grenade sitting dormant inside me."

"I think in this case, your father proved

that being a sociopath makes that easy." She looked at her hands. "You're a lot of things, Matias Javier Hernandez Balcazar. But a sociopath isn't one of them."

The ghost of a smile touched the corners of his mouth. "You know I wish that felt like an accomplishment."

She touched his hand. "Maybe someday it will."

"Maybe. You have very neatly turned this around. I wanted to know why you were a virgin."

"All I have is speculation." But she knew that was a lie. It was a knot in her brain that she hadn't yet unspooled, not even for herself. But she decided that she would try. For him. For her. Because they were both different here. There was no one to perform for. They just got to be. They got to breathe. "Maybe the truth is in what you just said. I didn't know how to want anything for myself. And then I met you. And there was something so… Compelling about you. And it isn't the way that the media talks about you. I found you to be so wholly different than what they said."

"The Pitbull."

"Yes. Anyone who thinks otherwise is an

idiot, in my opinion. Or they just haven't looked into your eyes."

"There's nothing there now."

"That's a lie. Whether you see it or not, I see so much there. And I wanted you. In a way that I never... I never wanted anyone like that before. I told myself it was because I wanted the fantasy of what we had that night. Because I felt beautiful. Because I felt... Special. Because I felt like the one being taken care of, instead of the other way around."

"And here you are being my seeing-eye dog."

"I don't see myself that way. It isn't that. It's not. I'm sorry. If I made you feel that way."

"Don't apologize to me. I'm not so easily wounded. I'm not even entirely certain that I have feelings."

"I think the problem is that you do. We both do. It doesn't mean we especially know what to do with them, but we both have them."

"It's a nice thing to think." She wondered which thing he meant.

That they both had a lot of feelings, or maybe that she connected with him in a way that she never had with anyone else. In a way that no one else had.

"I didn't even know what wanting someone felt like," she said. "I understand what attraction feels like. Not the need to act on it. Not until you."

"Why me?"

"Maybe we are the same," she said.

"How?" He sounded completely uncertain, but not angry, not derisive.

"The way that we've built walls around ourselves in order to survive. The way that we became other people. I don't know that I was conscious of becoming another person. I don't think it was a decision in quite the same way yours was."

"You're like me before," he said slowly. "A creation of my surroundings. There was no decision made. It was only after, when I decided to become an entirely new thing."

She nodded. "I didn't do that. I stayed the same. I just move myself. But nothing else changed. This was different. You were different. Reaching outside of myself, rather than wandering around trying to be self-contained."

"I'm not certain that I'm worthy of any of this."

"It's not about you," she said. "Well, it is. It's about you creating a response in me, I suppose. But acting on it… That was for me. In the very best way."

"Well, I am pleased for you then."

"We are naked in a field," she said. "I think maybe we're both the same kind of fool."

"Is it foolish to want someone, do you think?"

"You should know. You're the playboy. Many more women have wanted you than men have wanted me, and certainly you wanted more women than I've ever wanted men."

"No. That is true. I have wanted sex in the same way a person wants a piece of cake. Wanting you is different."

"Oh."

"It is like the moment where the air is caught between winter and spring. The last week before school lets out for the holidays. The longing for something, so specific and sharp it takes your breath away. I cannot say it better than that."

"Well," she breathed. "I don't think I can say anything better than that."

She moved closer to him, her bare skin touching his. And she let the sun warm them both. It was a long time before they went back inside.

And when she led him back upstairs, and to his bed, she went with him.

Because for the first time in a very long

time, she wasn't simply moving forward. She was still.

She intended to feel everything in this still-ness. Because it was probably the only time this was ever going to happen.

CHAPTER TWELVE

THE NEXT DAY she became a taskmaster. All night she had been pliant and beautiful in his arms. And now that night and day were all the same to him, the hours bled into one another seamlessly. Time had stopped meaning anything. There was only the darkness, and Auggie. He could not say that he minded it. But then she became a little taskmaster. Forcing him to memorize the layouts of the different rooms.

"This is not permanent," he said as he stood at the threshold of what she had informed him was the living room, trying to make him navigate his way into the kitchen. "Neither my lack of sight, nor staying here."

"But it is now," Auggie pointed out. "It is the reality we're both living in. And I don't want you to break your neck."

"You are much happier when I'm breaking your back."

He heard her sputtering, blustering, and he really did wish that he could see her expression.

"That is a crude thing to say."

"I rather thought it was clever."

"You are an enigma. Because sometimes you are still that…shameless, charming playboy, and then other times you are…"

"A black hole of impenetrable darkness?"

"Yes," she said. "That."

"Maybe both things are true. Maybe both men are me. Though, I don't know if I can figure out how to join the two together. I don't know if I would want to."

"I don't know. I like both."

She liked him. She liked him. He turned that over within himself. He couldn't recall a woman ever *liking* him before, not the real him. What a strange thing.

He was used to the world having a favorable opinion of him. To being regarded as a highly likable person, but he knew that it was fake. Because he knew that he was fake. She knew something else about him, and she seemed fond of him anyway. She was still here.

"Why are you here with me?"

"Where else would I go, Matias?"

"Back to your real life?"

"This is my real life right now. You are my real life."

"Because you are an endless martyr to your need to care for other people?" That was possibly taking it too far. But she had cared for her mother as a teenager, and it was entirely possible that it was what drove her now. She had said herself. They were all walking altars to their own trauma, after all.

"No," she said. "It's about me. It's about... The sex, frankly. I feel more in touch with myself than I have in a very long time, and actually, I would've told you that were I faced with another situation where I had to take care of somebody having a medical issue, I would run fifty miles. To get away from it. To get away from them. But it doesn't feel the same. I want to be here. With you. Don't let it go to your head."

"My ego is as big as it can possibly get."

"That isn't true at all. You are the most self-loathing person wrapped in a cloak of false ego that I have ever met."

Her words struck him. And he decided that he was done talking. So he went on navigating through the kitchen. And he managed to do it without running into too many things. Though part of him resisted the exercise, because he was not going to become accustomed to blindness. It was not a permanent state.

In that he was determined.

She continued to work him like that for the week. But at night, she went to bed with him, and the intimacy that they built there was like a glimmering kingdom. He might not be able to see anything, but that had become more real to him than anything else ever had. It was the only reality he cared to lose himself in.

They could have called in staff, but he was resistant to it, and she didn't seem to mind. She was the one who had to do all of the work in the absence of anyone there to cook for them. Because he was at such a disadvantage. But he found himself growing in his trust for her.

He couldn't recall ever having trusted another person before. Growing up with a father like his, he had only ever been able to trust himself. Especially with the way he had pitted him and his sister against each other.

He was good. She was bad.

It had only made him want to protect her, to be better to keep the focus off of her. It had made him feel like...like he had to be hard on her sometimes so his father wouldn't be.

Like he could protect her with his correction because he actually did care.

It had ended badly anyway.

He navigated his way into the kitchen, listening to the sounds of her moving around. Something was cooking, and it smelled good.

"Nothing fancy," she said. "Just some soup and bread."

"That sounds sufficient."

As he stood there, surrounded by a hominess that was completely unfamiliar to him, he felt as if he might be willing to make this trade. His sight for this life. This normalcy that was so beyond anything he had ever known.

Of course, she was having to take care of him, and she might feel different. He was potentially a burden to her, no matter what she said.

The girl who had been running away from this for so many years.

"Sufficient," she said. "Don't hurt yourself with compliments."

"Of course I was being dry."

"I know," she said. He could hear the warmth in her voice.

"I made a fire in the parlor; I thought we might sit in there and enjoy the warmth and the soup."

"You put a lot of thought into it." It was a bland thing to say, and yet there was nothing bland about it. The realization that she had done this for him. That she seemed to put effort and thought into this care.

"It feels like… Like reliving another life here."

"Agreed."

"I'm going to dish everything and bring it into the parlor. Do you think you can find your way?"

He paused, and oriented himself in the room. He found his touchpoints, and then he figured out which way he needed to go to make it into the next room, locating his path and making his way there slowly.

There would be a time when he wasn't entirely dependent on her to take care of him. He was getting better.

Do you want to get better at this?

This was the strangest thing of all. He wasn't living his life. The life he had been living for all these years. One of endless revenge.

No. He was… Living life. In a way that he never had before. In a way he had never thought he might want to.

But this wasn't him. It wasn't anything he

had earned. He had to stay wounded in order to stay with her. It was a strange dichotomy.

He moved carefully to his chair, feeling the warmth of the fire. He took a seat, and heard her walk into the room.

"I have a tray with two bowls on it, soup and bread."

She was telling him so that he knew what to picture. But he didn't care about the food. Instead, he thought of Auggie herself.

Tried to picture her face as it might be right now. The strongest image of her was of how she had looked the last night he had seen her. When they had been together as lovers for the first time. He had touched her countless times since, and had tried to memorize each dip and hollow of her body with his fingertips.

But he missed her face.

"What are you wearing today, Auggie?"

She chuckled. "You used to actively avoid calling me by my nickname."

"It's a silly name."

He heard her set the tray down on the table. "Hold your hands out," she said.

She placed the bowl of soup in his hands.

"I agree," she said. He heard her settle down, heard the clanking of her spoon on her bowl. "It is a silly name. I wanted very badly to be called Gus. That, I thought at least was a bit edgy. Sort of a nice, boyish name. Auggie sounds like somebody's pet dog."

"That isn't quite what I thought. But a valid concern."

She laughed. "I got used to it. It's just what stuck. There's not much you can do about that. I always wonder what my mother was thinking, though."

He took a cautious bite of soup. It was sweet and spicy. There was a hint of curry to it.

"Curried sweet potato," she said. Which made him aware that he must've made a face, and she had responded to it.

"Very good," he said.

"Thank you."

"Your mother was always single?"

"Yes," said Auggie. "She never married. She didn't give me any details about my father, not really. I mean I know I could do a DNA test or something, and find out more about him, but part of me is hesitant to do that. Once you open Pandora's box you can't close it again. What if he's married, I mean, what if he was married when they got together? Or what if he's a bad person? Or what if he's dead. And then it's just more grief that I didn't have to sign on for."

"I don't blame you for that," he said. "Life has proven to me that it is more often cruel than not."

"I'm not sure that's my takeaway. But I'm also not sure that I want to take on any more family members."

"You had a lonely childhood."

He felt her stillness. The way that it shifted the air around her when he said that.

"Yes," she said slowly. "I did. I knew other kids who had very strict parents. Who had to be mature because there was some expectation being put on them. Because their mother or father didn't really like them being children. But that wasn't what happened with my mother. She needed me to be there for her. She didn't want that, but at the same time, I think she was very grateful that she had a daughter who could help take care of her. Her own mother lived far away and wasn't able to help care for her. She died before my mother did. There was just no one else in her life."

She paused, and he heard her shift in her chair. "It's funny I… I feel like talking to you about your past, it's making me think of mine differently. I always had the feeling that she had made a lot of decisions that put her in a very lonely place, and that she regretted it, but I didn't know how to talk to her about it. I was caught in a place where I still saw her as my mother, and therefore not only human, not fully frail. But she was. I did my best to be there for her, but it meant not being there for myself. But I had limited time with her, so... It isn't like I could have deferred caring for her until I was older. And if not me... It would've been just home care nurses, and a rotating group of them at that. It wouldn't have been the same. And how much better would my life be if I was off at homecoming or prom instead of at home watching movies with her. They're memories I don't have the chance to make up for again."

She sighed heavily. "And she really was a wonderful mother. She did everything she could. She tried. We went for walks in the evening when the weather was nice, even when she didn't have a lot of energy. She told me that I was smart, and that I was brave. I was lonely, but I often don't think that I really have the right to be. Because she was there for me. It's just not the same as having friends and toys and a social life. It's not the same as having easy. I think you can have a life filled with all kinds of different love. And when you're a child often that love is free of responsibility. It's easy. I never really got to experience that love. For me, it always held responsibility."

Something tore at him. This image of a child who didn't know what it was to have a love that didn't have cost. He was not often moved by other people's stories, his own was so difficult, it was often difficult for him to find empathy.

But not now. She got beneath his skin. She touched him.

He knew exactly what that was like. To never have love or care feel like something you could take for granted. He knew what that was like. All too well.

He felt undone by this. By the heavy feeling in his chest. She hadn't chosen that life, and she had emerged from it strong.

So many children were born into loving, easy families. But not her. Not him.

If she hadn't chosen this, then perhaps he...

He pushed that aside.

"What about your mother?" she asked.

He paused. "I... I don't even know how to talk about my mother. She is still living. I never hear from her. I guess you could say she was never a major influence in my life. My father took control of everything, my mother sat back quietly. She spent his money…she gave him his heirs. I'm not angry at her. I'm not. She can't even grieve her own daughter properly because he won't allow it, because he says she can't cry for a person who caused their own death. He owns even her thoughts, and I can only pity her. I am not angry with her."

He sat there for a moment, and wondered if that was true.

But their father had not abused them with fists. He had ruled over them, had manipulated them. But their lives hadn't been in danger. In truth, they had all been like frogs slowly boiling in water.

"Were you ever happy?"

"I never thought about it. I just… Lived. As any child does." He was silent for a moment. "Were you?"

"I suppose it was the same for me. I didn't think much about whether or not it was all difficult until it was over. No. That isn't true. Toward the end it all got very hard. And knowing, I think that it would end I started just wishing that it would. It made me feel… Terrible. Once she was gone. Like I had made it happen faster. Like I had been impatient, selfish."

"No one wants to watch someone they

love die. I understand. I..." It was very hard for him to get out the words that he needed to speak now. "My sister was lost in her addiction for a long time. I worried about that phone call. The one that we eventually got. There was a time when I did treat her as if she was fragile. And then I got angry. And my father's anger fueled me. I forgot my fear. Because part of me just thought... If it happened, then I would be able to move on. That I would be able to live. Without thinking of her all the time. Without worrying all the time. The first thought that I had when I found out she had overdosed was that at least I didn't have to worry about her anymore."

That tore at him. It made his stomach ache. It made him feel like he was falling. And surely she would tell him what a monster he was. Because it was a monstrous thing to think. It was. Truly.

"I understand," she said. "I do. When my mother died... The night that she was the most poorly, I gave her pain medication, and I went to bed. I woke up at four in the morning. She was gone. And I felt... Relief. It was like all the breath left my body, and like everything that was tying me to that town, to that house, was suddenly just released. The worry.

I didn't realize how much worry I carried. Because every time we would think she was getting better, I would just find out later that she wasn't. Waiting for test results. Waiting for everything. And I hadn't realized how much it was weighing me down. And of course if I had a choice I would choose to keep her. Of course I would. But nobody gave me that choice. So in the end... In the end, there was something easier about just being free."

"Do you still feel free?" he asked, his voice rough.

"I don't know. Not every day. I feel like I don't recognize myself sometimes. Like the life that I live now is so different from the life I had then it's like I'm someone new."

"I don't feel free," he said. "Because in that one moment when I realized that I was happy, I didn't have to worry about my sister anymore, I also realized that I was the one that had pushed her. I was the one that had done it. I was the difference between her staying and going. And I could've changed the entire time, but I didn't. Because I didn't know how. Because... My entire foundation is rotten, but that is not an excuse. It just isn't."

"Why isn't it? You didn't choose to have the parents that you had. Neither did she."

"No. But it… I don't want to think about it anymore."

It was too painful. All of this. Just too damned painful.

"We don't have to. Tell me one good memory from your childhood."

He laughed. "That's the problem. There are no good memories. Not anymore. It's just… Everything that was good is now sustained by grief."

"No. It's like this. Like this moment, completely taken out of time. Remove it from time. Nothing came before, nothing came after. Tell me."

He took a deep breath. He didn't have to close his eyes to block anything out. And he could see in his mind, a clear view of the olive groves, of the cypress trees that he and his sister used to ride horses through. The only time that they were free. "I remember being young with my sister. Pretending we were vagabonds. That we were running away. We would pack up green apples and bread, and put them in a pillowcase, and ride our horses until we reached the edge of the family estate." He could see it so clearly. The horizon stretching out before them. There had never been a wall there. But they had acted like

there was. Like that boundary was impass-
able. "I don't know why we didn't just keep
going. We should have."

They had built a fence with their own
minds. But it had been as real as it needed to
be. It had kept them in line. Their father had
created it with his cruelty. With the control
that he exerted on all of them. He had waged
a battle with their minds when they had been
only children, and he had won.

Does he still wage that same battle?

But then, she was there, putting her hand
over his, and he could feel the warmth of her
body, could taste her breath. It was sweet,
and lovely just like she was. And when she
pressed her soft mouth to his, he allowed
that warmth, that need, that desire to spread
through his entire body. This was real. Everything else… It could wait. Everything else…
It didn't matter. No. How could it? This time
out from his real life felt like the most con-
sequential thing he had ever experienced. He
could not explain it. He would not try.

Instead, he just let her kiss him. Instead he
just pulled her onto his lap, and saw his way
into her beauty with his fingertips. Moving
them over her soft face, down her back. He
pulled her shirt up over her head, and then un-

hooked her bra with deft skill. He stripped her bare and learned her every curve. He moved his hands down her hips, and then pushed one between her legs, feeling how wet with need she was. That she could see him like this and still want him, that she could hear those pathetic stories from his childhood and still be like this…

He was grateful, and even that made him feel like less, but when her mouth rained kisses down upon his face, his neck, when she pulled his shirt up over his head, and continued down to kiss his chest, down his abs, he did not feel anything like pathetic. And yet at the same time this did not feel like a return to the man he had been. It did not feel like the real wakening of a playboy. It felt like something entirely new. Something he had not yet experienced before.

She slid off of his lap, and he could feel that she came to rest on the floor between his legs. Her hands moved to his belt, where she undid that, and the closure on his slacks. She pulled his pants down just slightly, freeing him. And then she leaned in, her mouth soft now on his shaft, her tongue making dark magic as she tasted him, as she took him into her mouth, sucked him deep.

He felt like pushing through the darkness inside him, and he wished… He wished that he could see her. Wished that he could see her with her head bent over his lap like this. Because he hadn't seen Auggie enough time since he had truly begun to see her, in ways that his eyes could never have comprehended. And now that was lost to him.

They had that night. That night when he had really understood, how beautiful she was, how singular she was. And all the times before that, he had been bringing women on his private jet, women who weren't her. He had been satiating himself on bread and water when there was a feast on the other side of the door. Because as lovely as those women were, they had not fit him in this way. It wasn't the same. There was something singular at work between himself and Auggie. He would've said that he was not capable of a singular connection. He would've said that he wasn't capable of connection at all.

That it was lost on him, wasted on him.

He had learned to feel one thing. The driving desire for revenge, and it blotted out everything else, but with her he had found something more. It was not the loss of his sight that had heightened his senses. It was her.

Knowing her, talking to her, feeling for her. Wanting to know her, rather than simply wanting satisfaction for the death of his sister. And he wanted to resist it, but here and now he simply couldn't. In the same way he couldn't resist her.

He had decided that he would no longer feel helpless. That was the thing. He had decided that there would be no more invisible fences. He had taken his life and fashioned it into whatever he wished it to be. He had fashioned himself into an instrument of revenge. He was not at the mercy of anything anymore. Not of his feelings, not of the way he wanted another person, but right now he was.

And he wanted to believe that it was all right, that he could have it because they were here, and he couldn't see. Because he was being forced to take a break from everything he was.

But it felt like something deeper than that. Felt like something more powerful.

And as she drove him to the brink with that clever mouth, he gave himself over to her.

In the same way he had given himself over to revenge all those years ago. Right now, in this moment, his only loyalty was to Auggie.

He was drowning. In her, in the sensation.

And just as he was about to be pushed over

the edge entirely he lifted her up and brought her down onto his lap. He found that she had nothing on beneath the skirt that she wore, and he found the glorious entrance to her body, and thrust home.

She gasped with need, and he drove up into her, pushing them both toward the ultimate end. Toward their glorious satisfaction. And when they both found their release, they clung to one another. And he knew something in the stillness that was almost like peace. He didn't want to move for fear he might shatter it. He didn't want to breathe for fear that it would prove to be only an illusion.

He held onto her. He was afraid to breathe.

She rested her head in the crook of his neck, and he put his hand on the back of her head, holding her there.

How long had it been since he had the chance to comfort another person. To be there for them. How long had it been since someone had done so for him, and in this moment they were doing it for one another.

He felt whole in a way he had not in so many years. Perhaps ever.

He wanted to sit there in that.

"We can do the dishes tomorrow," she whispered. "Let's just go to bed."

He nodded in agreement. And he let her take his hand. Allowed her to lead him up the stairs, because it felt good to let someone care for him. Because it felt good to be cared for. Because for some reason he had the deep and certain sensation that this was a very fragile thing. And that when it broke there would be nothing that could be done to stop it. And so when he went to bed with her that night, it was with the knowledge that the dawn wasn't guaranteed. Nor anything afterward.

And the last thought he had before he drifted off to sleep was that losing her would never be a relief.

Because this was something he had never known before. A weight and responsibility that felt like joy. And he had no idea what to call it.

No idea what to do with any of it.

He was satisfied.

Without his sight, without his revenge, in this out-of-the-way manor, hiding away from the world, Matias Balcazar finally understood what it was like to have everything.

CHAPTER THIRTEEN

LAST NIGHT HAD been transformative. Truly.
Auggie was still pondering it the next day.
She had been pondering it the entire time. Not
only her changing feelings toward him, but the
situation they found themselves in here. She
knew that she needed to talk to him about…
About potentially making a statement. But she
hated the idea of bringing the outside in at all.
It had been two weeks, and he wasn't better.
He was going to have to go see the neurologist, and even though there was still a lot of
hope as far as restoring his sight, it was all…
It was all converging. The need to handle the
headlines, the need to make intervention with
his health… All of it.

Your feelings.

True. But her feelings could wait.

She stared down at her hands, where she
had them pressed to the top of the kitchen
counter. Her feelings. Did she love him. What

even was love? She had never been certain. Maybe that was why she had never really wanted it. Maybe it was why it was easy to avoid men and desire and all of those things because she couldn't imagine love in a way that didn't feel heavy.

And this did feel heavy, but it was different.

He made her feel supported. He made her feel like she mattered.

He listened to her. He was like a different person than the one that she had met initially. Not just because she had gotten to the bottom of that dark wound that existed beneath the playboy veneer. But she had also found parts of him that were less intense. Parts of him that were giving, rather than selfish. He was in fact a very deep thinker, which she had always known. But she realized it was why he committed so hard to the other version of himself.

Because his own deep thinking often hurt him.

His memories of his sister were still so vivid. His grief at losing her complex. It mirrored her own. She had never imagined that she would have something in common with him. She had more than something in common with him, in fact. She had a spirit that recognized his. A deep wound that saw his and recognized it. Deeper than empathy.

Or maybe this was just… Her wanting to keep on living in a fantasy. Maybe she was dangerously deluded. Maybe this was what everyone thought. That they had a unique connection with him. That he was most especially their brilliant and perfect lover. That while he might've touched other women it could never have been this.

Maybe that was an easy lie to tell herself.

She couldn't be certain.

But when he came downstairs, maneuvering slowly on his own, she felt it burst inside of her like a firework. That certainty.

She wanted to spend the rest of her life with him. It was now a clearer goal than anything else ever had been. It didn't erase the other things that she wanted. It didn't mean she no longer cared about her business, she did. It didn't mean she no longer carried baggage from her childhood, or felt a strange amount of anxiety regarding any proximity to her childhood. She did.

But there was room for this. Room for him.

To want something more than success, to want something more than distance from her past. To want something more than to simply succeed on her own. That was what she had been chasing all this time, a sense that she would be okay on her own because the crushing feeling of being left to her own devices seemed inevitable. She had always known that her mother would die young. Ever since she could understand the implications of the kind of cancer she had, Auggie had understood that.

That isolation. She had seen that the potential for that existed. They had had an accident. He was mortal. He had been injured. There were complications from that injury and they might continue.

But that reality didn't seem bigger than the hope that they could have something together.

She loved him.

She couldn't say anything right now. She had to sit with it. Because Auggie was the sort of girl that needed a plan.

"I was thinking," she said. "That since we have to go into the hospital to see the neurologist, it is probably time for you to put out a statement about your sister."

He paused. "I thought you said it was better to not engage in PR."

"What I think is better is maybe you saying something real about it. I don't think you should go through your publicist. I think you should just tell the truth. No spin."

"No spin?"

"Yes. What if you told the world the story of your sister. The way you told me. And maybe it's messy and you're not universally loved in the end."

"I never cared about being universally loved."

"Didn't you?"

She wondered if maybe he had, in a way. If part of him had craved that because he had never gotten it anywhere else.

"I suppose it was better than being a disappointment. But that was never the goal."

"No. It was to show your father that he was wrong in every way. But... Maybe the truth does that more effectively. You loved Seraphina. Flaws and all. You loved her even though it was difficult. You're a better man than your father. It's evident just in that."

He tented his fingers beneath his chin. "I don't know how to talk about my feelings."

"We've been doing a lot of it since we've been here."

"But this doesn't count." He waved his hand in a sweeping gesture, and she felt like he had taken all her chess pieces off the table in one fell swoop. Because he had just dismissed this entire experience. This experience that had been so profound to her.

He doesn't mean it that way.

She bit her bottom lip. "Well, maybe it'll count for something."

"Once we leave here, Auggie, you're not obligated to me. You never were."

"Yes. I could've just left you blind and stumbling around."

"You could have."

She could have. It was a strange thing, actually, to really sit with that reality. There hadn't been anything stopping her. She could have done that. She could have.

She could have.

That was actually true of her caring for her mother too. She felt like she had had no other choice. But she had.

But when things had gotten hard, that was how she had chosen to love her mother.

She felt like realization had just exploded within her.

She had chosen to do the hard thing because her love was strong.

She had seen herself as sort of a victim of it. Of her circumstances.

But he was right. She had chosen this.

"You're right," she said. "I could've walked

away. But I didn't. Because I... I care about you."

He looked at her, even though he could not see her. Those dark eyes landed on her unerringly. "You shouldn't."

He said it so final. Heavy. Like he'd set a stone on her chest.

He didn't want her to care.

This was how it was going to be. He was going to resist this. All the way.

No matter the conversations they'd had, no matter the way that she knew him. No matter that she had been trying to show him that he could have a life apart from pursuing revenge against his father, he was going to make this impossible.

"Let's go," she said.

"To?"

"The doctor. And the paparazzi might come after us. But I believe that my work wives have planted a story about us jetting off to St. Tropez. It is also entirely possible that your private jet is making a decoy flight there."

"Genius," he said.

"If nothing else it should get us out of here and to the hospital without being inundated. And then perhaps we can sneak back to your town house."

"I had just learned how to live here."

She felt that. All the way down to her bones.

She packed up anything important, the clothing that had been sent for her, and any remaining food, and put it in the back of the new car that had been delivered for them a few days earlier.

She was tasked with driving them back to the city. She wasn't entirely comfortable with driving on the other side of the road, but she managed, and navigated them to the doctor.

They did a scan of his brain, and the neurologist explained that he still had fluid pushing against his optic nerves.

"The best thing to do would be to go in and drain it."

"That sounds hideous," she said.

"Whatever will work," he said.

"We can do surgery tomorrow morning. Do you wish to stay here tonight?"

"No," he said.

She tried not to put too much stock in that. That he had made the choice that would allow them to be together. That would allow them to be together this last night.

Last night? Nothing is going to happen to him.

Maybe not. But if this fixed his vision, he

wouldn't need her around anymore. It would be revenge, as usual. And his reputation… Well. It was going to take more than an engagement for her to fix it. It was going to take the truth. And he was going to have to find it in himself to be somewhat… Real. She knew he could do it. The question was, would he?

When they returned to his London home, he made love with her like the clock was ticking. It was. She understood that.

And then she couldn't hold it any longer. She looked at him, watching her fingertips drift over his face. What a familiar sight he was to her. But she wouldn't be to him.

"I love you, Matias."

And then everything broke apart.

CHAPTER FOURTEEN

HE DIDN'T KNOW what to say to that. There was no joy in it. There was... Nothing but pain. She was offering him something that felt like treasure, but he could not reach out and grab it.

It was darkness. All of it was darkness.

Because he didn't deserve this. He didn't want it. How could he?

How could he when he was... He was responsible for all of this. For the loss of his sister. He didn't deserve to absolve himself of it. He didn't deserve to have that surgery tomorrow to have everything fixed.

They were going to cut his brain open. Perhaps he would bleed out on the table. Perhaps that would be the ultimate justification. What had not finished him during the accident would finish him then.

She couldn't love him.

"Auggie… If I have given you the impression that this was something that it wasn't…"

"Don't. Don't be the charming playboy. Don't lie to me. Don't deflect."

That made him angry. "I'm trying to be kind to you."

"You cannot break someone's heart kindly, Matias. Do it with honesty. Do one damn thing with honesty. Do you even know what that is anymore?"

"I… I damn well do. I know that the honest truth is my life is a mess of my own making. And if I never managed to clean it up it will be my just desserts."

"That's a lie. It just is. And I don't know if you're telling it just to me, or to yourself as well, but it is a lie. You loved your sister. Do you know how I know? Because you feel that great and terrible grief. The one that is nothing simple. Loving her hurts as much as losing her, and that is love. Hard and sharp and nothing simple. You would never have chosen to lose her. You would do anything to fix it. Look at you. You have sacrificed your entire life in the name of trying to fix it in some fashion. You are heartbroken, and that tells me everything I need to know about you. About whether or not you're actually worthy of anything."

MILLIE ADAMS   231

"No, I… It doesn't matter. There is one thing. One thing that I'm here for. One thing that I was put on this earth to do in the wake of losing her."

He was scrambling to find new reasons. To find a new way to push her back.

Because what she was offering was… It was too painful. Too bright. A light pushing through the darkness, and he was far too accustomed to the darkness.

Far too accustomed to the mess that he had made of himself. The facsimile of a human being he had created. His body was one he simply existed in. His soul was long since gone.

He had never been his own person. He had been a creation of his father…

He still was.

All of this was his father's doing. Every last bit of it. From him going to shame his sister for drug use, to this. All of it. The blindness. The accident. He was his father's creation. And that was worse than being at fault for the death of his sister. A mindless drone who walked the earth for no other reason than that that man had created him. Physically, and emotionally.

He was nothing more. And Auggie was…

She was everything. She knew herself. Truly. She lived a life that helped make things better for other people. She had loved her mother in a real intentional way. That she had created a life that outshone his own in every way.

He had never felt like less. And he could not respond to this thing that she was giving to him.

"Auggie, I am not the man you should give that to. I have never proven that I could be more than my father's pawn."

"So what? You'll die that way because you started that way?"

"Maybe. Maybe that's the generational curse. Maybe it's the best thing that can happen. My father's line will end with him. Whether I live long or short, perhaps that is the best way for it to be."

"No. I'm not having this. I'm not listening."

"I have surgery tomorrow and I cannot see, and I am not myself and…"

"You are yourself. You were the most yourself that you had ever been. This last week, that was a taste of it. Of living. Why can't you choose that?"

"Because it is not that simple."

"No. This is you riding to the edge of the

property and stopping, because you feel that there is a fence there even though there isn't."

Her words were like a shotgun blast.

Fences that were never really there.

Was he destined always to live that way.

"Maybe you're right," he said. "But I will always see them."

"You can't see anything. You had a chance. To have it all wiped away. That was what we were just living. Your clean slate. Even your vision was taken away, and you still choose to see the fences. I can't fix that for you."

He heard her get out of bed. Heard her dressing.

"I will send someone for you in the morning, but it isn't going to be me. I need to take care of myself. I need… I need to breathe."

He didn't argue. But he wanted to. He wanted her to stay with him. Desperately. Because he had never felt alone in this darkness until she walked out of the room. Until he heard her walk out of the house. And then he felt hopeless. Then he truly felt the loss of control. Then it really felt like he would die of this.

Without her. Without his vision. Without everything.

He had known on some level that he would have to stay wounded to stay with her.

Or maybe you have to heal. Maybe you have to push through this. Push past it.

But what was on the other side? Those fences might be made up, but he still couldn't see beyond them.

Make a statement that's real. Make one that's from your heart.

She had told him to do that. To make a statement about his sister that was the honest truth.

But right now... He had never been more aware that he could not see. And it was not a lack of sight that made that true.

CHAPTER FIFTEEN

AUGGIE WAS IN misery and regretting every decision that she had made. From telling him that she was in love with him to leaving him.

And when she dragged herself into the Your Girl Friday headquarters she didn't bother to hide any of her regret.

"Auggie," Lynna said, looking shocked. "You're back."

"I am."

"No one else is here. They all have jobs."

"Right. Well. I'm here. And everything is terrible."

The story of what happened with Matias poured out of her, and she wasn't quite sure what to expect of Lynna as far as reactions went.

But there was no judgment.

"So what are you going to do?"

"What can I do? He made his position on all of this really clear."

"It's true. But you don't have to listen to him."

"It makes you kind of pathetic to keep going after a guy who said he didn't want you."

"He didn't say he didn't want you. And anyway, I don't know. I think people should be willing to be a little bit pathetic for love. Isn't that the point of it? I mean, I certainly wouldn't bother with it if it wasn't. So maybe I never will. But…"

"No. Everyone is supposed to be balanced and healthy and not ask too much of each other, and not need each other too much."

"What a boring reality."

Auggie found she couldn't disagree. She didn't want quiet or reserved. She didn't even mind this breaking her open, because it had helped her find new parts of herself.

She didn't want to end up without him, however. But at the same time… She just wanted him.

And she wanted to be this version of herself that had blossomed with him.

So maybe there was something in all this.

"He's going into surgery soon. I won't be able to make it to the hospital in time to see him beforehand."

"You should probably go anyway. Because

the way you feel about him isn't really contingent on how he feels about you, is it?"

With that truth, Auggie took her bruised heart down to the hospital. She was informed that he was in surgery. But told that she would be updated when he was finished.

Her phone buzzed in her pocket, and she pulled it out, seeing that she had a text from Irinka.

Was this your doing?

She frowned, and opened up the link that Irinka had sent.

It was a statement. From Matias.

He must've dictated it to someone last night after she left. Before he went into surgery.

She sat there, holding the phone, her mouth agape as she read.

Augusta Fremont encouraged me to make this statement before she left me in the early hours of the morning. She is another person that I have failed. But that is not the point of this statement.

By now rumors, planted by my father have run rampant that I am responsible for the death of my sister.

I have spent my life feeling that I was responsible. It is why I live the way that I do. But always, always I wanted to destroy my father with my success. I blamed us both for her death. My own harsh words that I spoke to her the last time I saw her, but also him, because he raised me to be that harsh, and because he raised her to feel so much shame.

It was the perfect counterpoint. I was the match, and she was gasoline. I have walked in guilt all these years, because it was more comfortable than grief. And it was not until I had an accident two weeks ago that forced me to sit and recover...it was not until I spent that time with a woman who showed me what life could be...that I began to see things for what they were. There were fences in my mind. Roadblocks that I was convinced were the real truth. She made me see that they weren't.

But I was not able to change my opinion on that truth until it was too late. I'm writing this ahead of brain surgery. I don't know how I will come out of it. The doctor made it sound as if it would be easy, but if I have learned one thing about life it's that things are rarely easy. Perhaps I did cause my sister to overdose. Perhaps she would've done it anyway. All I know is I live with the grief either way. And blame and revenge felt active in a way that the loss of her doesn't. Living in anger and regret has felt much more manageable than living in hope. Than wanting to find a joy and love that I never truly had in my life.

I manufactured fake joy and kept it all around myself. I cultivated a persona in the media that allowed me to bask in the warmth of fake flames, so that I could know at least a fraction of what it was like to be cared for. After having someone give me love for real, I recognize that it isn't enough. She told me to be real. And I am. I have no answers. Only pain. I cannot bring my sister back. I can only grieve her. If I destroy my father, nothing will be rebuilt. And that too is pointless. The only thing that has not felt pointless is the hope that it gave me to have someone love me.

To begin to fall in love with her. I'm clinging to that hope now, because now that I've got a taste for it, I fear it might be the one thing I have ever been well and truly addicted to.

And that is all thanks to her.

Whatever this means for my future, for my company, for my place in the tabloids, I don't care. I care about Auggie and the truth, in that order. The truth is that I love her. The truth is that I'm still figuring out what love is.

And so, however I come out of my surgery tomorrow, with my sight or without, having lost motor skills or not, it is the one thing that will be true about me. I am not a creation of my father's. I am not a man who has everything. I am not the best beloved playboy in the world. I am not a golden retriever. All of those things are fake.

But loving Auggie is real.

A tear splashed down on her phone screen. It was a statement that wasn't going to do anything for him. It was a personal revelation, and nothing more. There were no neat bows. And the public didn't like that.

But it mattered to her. It echoed inside of her. As real as anything had ever been.

Irinka sent another text.

What exactly is happening?

He loves me.

He loved her, and she had to wait for him to wake up.

She needed him to wake up. But she didn't need him to be physically perfect. She would care for him. She would stay with him.

You are going to marry a billionaire and abandon our business, are you?

No. I mean, I might marry a billionaire. But I'll always be your work wife.

Work Wives Forever.

A man in scrubs entered the room. "He did well. He woke up talking."

"And his vision?"

"Come and see him. And let him see you."

On shaking legs she walked into the recovery room. And there he was, his head leaned back against the pillow. Looking alarmingly handsome in spite of everything.

His eyes fluttered open and came to rest on her. He could see her. She knew that he could.

"Auggie," he said. "I hope that I can see and that this isn't a dream. I hope that you're here."

"I'm here."

"You came for me. You saw what I wrote."

"I did. But not until I was already here. Because… Just because you sent me away didn't mean I didn't love you. And I needed to be here for this. I had to."

"That is more than I deserve."

"It's how I love. Fierce and tough and forever."

"I don't know how I love," he said. "I haven't even been certain of what it is until... Until you. I am afraid that it is hard and complicated. But it will take a long time for me to figure out how to get it just right. But I want to try, Auggie. I want a life. Not a mission. I want picnics. And smell the flowers. And to live. I want to be my own, but most of all I want to be yours."

"You're just saying that because you're so happy you can see."

"To be honest, I cared about that less than I could've imagined except... I wanted to see your face. I wanted to see your face since I fell in love with you. And you are even more beautiful than I remembered."

She closed the distance between them and went to his bedside. She reached out and took his hand and pressed her cheek against it. "Now you really are delirious. I haven't slept and I look like garbage."

"No. You are the most beautiful thing that I have ever seen. And I am seeing you really. For the first time. Because I really do see it now. I was running from pain, but you can't run from that. Guilt and anger were preferable to missing her. To mourning a childhood I did not choose. But if you didn't choose it then neither did I. These hard things… They just are. You are a living testament to the fact that it is what you do after that matters. You did so much more with your hand than I did with mine. I want to be like you. And maybe I will not be a simple character for the world anymore. But I will be a real person. And that is infinitely better, I think."

"I love you."

"I love you too."

EPILOGUE

The Pitbull puppies are on board.

MATIAS SENT THAT text to his wife's group chat, even though the women were just outside in the waiting room. He smiled to himself as he looked down at his beautiful bride and the two babies she held in her arms.

Twins. He had never imagined so much joy.

A boy and a girl.

He had thought that he was destined to live a life alone. To live without love. And ever since he and Auggie had gotten married it had been nothing but the most pure influx of love he could've imagined.

He had been given his sight back. In more ways than he had realized he needed to have it restored.

"What are you on about?" she asked, looking at him.

"I was just letting everyone know that the babies are here."

"Thank you," she said, smiling up at him. "For everything."

He laughed. "What do you mean? You have given me my entire life."

"Well, that's kind of our whole thing. White glove service."

"This is definitely above and beyond."

"We aim to please."

"And that, my love, you have done."

* * * * *

*Read on for a sneak preview
of Millie Adams's*
Royally Pregnant,
for Harlequin Presents.

PRINCE ADONIS ANDREADIS HAD ALWAYS known that his wedding would be a magnificent spectacle. A man of his wealth and stature could have nothing other than a glorious and singular occasion to mark his nuptials. Even if those nuptials existed only to secure the bloodline, and therefore access to the throne of his country.

It was just he hadn't expected to feel anything about it.

His father was dying. There was no denying the reality.

His father had told him that he had done enough damage to the crown and the family reputation that he owed him a marriage minted in perfection.

Adonis couldn't disagree.

What Adonis knew was that he had done a fair job of exorcising his demons in the form of debauchery, all around the globe.

And while he had not intended to besmirch the crown, it was likely he had.

Well. Besmirch in the eyes of citizens his father's age. The younger generation was...decidedly fond of his exploits. He was a meme.

Knowing his time as king was on the horizon, he'd agreed to his father's demand. That he marry a suitable woman. His father had provided him with a folio of acceptable women.

He had spent years being a terrible playboy but even he had never chosen women off of a menu.

He couldn't say he felt like he owed his father, so much as he owed his country. His years of debauchery had never been intended to cause strife for the citizens of Olympus. No, his target had been much more personal.

The end result, however, was his infamy.

Adored by the youths, decried by the elder generation.

He had to find a way to unite the two schools of thought, however. And marrying seemed the way to do that.

He'd chosen Drusilla Stalworth not because of any blinding attraction to her, or her profile in the folio provided by his father, but because she was American royalty. The granddaughter of a former president, the daughter of a billionaire business mogul.

He had decided to reform, to forge an appropriate alliance and to marry as quickly as possible. His decisions had been clear, concise and quick.

He couldn't recall deciding to get married in a cathedral by the sea, however. But it seemed as if that's what he was doing.

The building was glass, glorious light shone through the windows.

It was warm. Odd. He'd expected it to be cold.

He looked out into the pews of the church. There was no audience. And for a moment he felt outside of himself. But he continued walking up to the front. And there he stood, waiting for his bride. The doors opened, and there she was. A halo of glorious gold. White.

Her hair was piled on top of her head, and a veil concealed her face.

She was like a floating confection. An angel.

Spun sugar and sweetness. So strange that he should have a visceral reaction to her, because he could not recall ever having a reaction like this to Drusilla in the past.

No. He had always been decidedly neutral on his intended, which had been fine with him.

She was beneficial. She didn't need to be anything else.

But now, the sight of her held him suspended.

It was like being reborn.

And then, he was certain he felt something bite his leg. He looked around the room, and was struck yet again by the fact that it was empty, except for himself and Drusilla.

He reached down and gripped his thigh. And there was warmth there.

He was confused.

Groggy.

Why?

Suddenly, the doors to the church blew open, and the wind was an icy blast. All the warmth from before faded away. And Drusilla kept on walking toward him. But then her veil blew off. And he looked into the eyes of a stranger.

As snow began to fall inside the chapel.

The chapel?

No. There was no chapel.

He wasn't in Cape Cod having a wedding. He wasn't…

Suddenly, everything around him fell away. And the wedding dress transformed itself to a parka. While the chapel became the vast wilderness.

And then, his vision went black.

And he tried to cast his mind back, to figure out exactly how he had gotten here…

*Don't miss the new Millie Adams romance
available wherever
Harlequin Presents books
and ebooks are sold.*